Advanced Introduction to Public Policy

Elgar Advanced Introductions are stimulating and thoughtful introductions to major fields in the social sciences and law, expertly written by the world's leading scholars. Designed to be accessible yet rigorous, they offer concise and lucid surveys of the substantive and policy issues associated with discrete subject areas.

The aims of the series are two-fold: to pinpoint essential principles of a particular field, and to offer insights that stimulate critical thinking. By distilling the vast and often technical corpus of information on the subject into a concise and meaningful form, the books serve as accessible introductions for undergraduate and graduate students coming to the subject for the first time. Importantly, they also develop well-informed, nuanced critiques of the field that will challenge and extend the understanding of advanced students, scholars and policy-makers.

Titles in the series include:

Advanced Introduction to

Public Policy

B. GUY PETERS

Maurice Falk Professor, University of Pittsburgh, USA

Elgar Advanced Introductions

Edward Elgar
PUBLISHING

Cheltenham, UK • Northampton, MA, USA

Published by
Edward Elgar Publishing Limited
The Lypiatts
15 Lansdown Road
Cheltenham
Glos GL50 2JA
UK

Edward Elgar Publishing, Inc.
William Pratt House
9 Dewey Court
Northampton
Massachusetts 01060
USA

A catalogue record for this book
is available from the British Library

Library of Congress Control Number: 2014957094

MIX
Paper from
responsible sources
FSC® C013056

ISBN 978 1 78195 576 5 (cased)
ISBN 978 1 78195 577 2 (paperback)
ISBN 978 1 78195 578 9 (eBook)

Typeset by Servis Filmsetting Ltd, Stockport, Cheshire
Printed and bound in Great Britain by T.J. International Ltd, Padstow

Contents

Tables

Preface

The study of public policy is understanding what governments do and their effects on citizens. Although policy analysis is central to that understanding, it is by no means a simple undertaking. From an academic perspective the analysis is complex because it involves multiple disciplines – political science, economics, law, sociology and philosophy, among others. These disciplines all provide insights into policy, but they also provide different and perhaps conflicting perspectives on policy issues. Therefore, making decisions about what are good answers to policy problems is difficult.

At a more practical level some of the same concerns about public policy emerge. Given all the different perspectives on policy and policymaking, how can decision-makers make good choices when they make the decisions that will shape policies? Can the analytics provided by academic discussions provide effective guidance for those decision-makers or are they better advised to rely on their own intuition and judgment? Although this book is directed primarily to an academic audience, I would not have written it if I did not believe that it was relevant for the real world. The academic models developed here and elsewhere in the literature are abstracted from reality, but they also illuminate that reality.

One way to consider policy analysis from both the academic and practical perspectives is to use a concept of policy design. The fundamental argument behind this perspective is that making policy is a design science very much like architecture and engineering. While the messiness of the political process involved in making policy makes such a perspective appear excessively optimistic, the analyst can still develop and attempt to implement more coherent designs of policy. Even if that designing fails, and few policies are adopted and implemented exactly as designed, beginning with a coherent conception of the policy is likely to produce a more coherent result.

There are a number of colleagues and friends who should be thanked for their part, some unknown to them, in the development of this volume. Perhaps the deepest debt goes to Stephen H. Linder, my colleague at Tulane University during the 1980s. We wrote several articles together on ideas of policy design, as well as on other aspects of policy studies. He was central to my thinking about policy as an exercise in designing and in attempting to understand the complex interaction among causation, action and evaluation in studying public policy. Steve, and my other colleagues at Tulane, were extremely important in helping me develop ideas about public policy, and governing more generally. At the same time I had the pleasure of working with several British policy scholars such as Richard Rose and Brian Hogwood, and there was an even stronger foundation for developing a perspective on public policy. Several former students at the University of Pittsburgh – notably John Hoornbeek and Patrik Marier – have also contributed directly and indirectly to the development of this book. Over the past several years I have learned a great deal from my colleague Philippe Zittoun at the University of Lyon. And last, but not least, I continue to profit from my personal and professional interactions with Jon Pierre. We have been working together for some years on issues of policy and governance, and that cooperation continues to be both fun and productive.

I cannot, of course, blame any of the above-named colleagues for any inadequacies of this book, although it would certainly have been less adequate without them. And thanks also to Alex Pettifer from Edward Elgar who has been both encouraging and patient.

1 Public policy: a design perspective

Introduction

Public policy is the set of activities that governments engage in for the purpose of changing their economy and society (see Peters, forthcoming). Some years ago Harold Lasswell (1936) defined politics as "Who Gets What". Lasswell was one of the first social scientists to study public policy in a systematic manner, and his definition of politics emphasizes that the political process is ultimately about producing benefits, and costs, for the members of the society. In other words, public policy ultimately is about the public. All the other things that we identify with politics – elections, legislative voting, bureaucracy and even the courts – are significant primarily because they contribute to making and implementing public policy.

Any number of traditional academic disciplines should be involved in the study of public policy. This book is oriented toward the politics of policy but economics, law, sociology and ethics also make important contributions to understanding how governments intervene in the economy and society, and these disciplines inevitably will make numerous appearances in the discussions here. In addition, various substantive areas of expertise such as public health, education and climatology are relevant for various policy areas. Thus, to understand public policy involves bringing together a range of information and expertise, all focused on changing conditions in the economy and society.

Even within political science there are alternative approaches to understanding how policy is made and implemented. For example, the conventional political science approach has been to use the policymaking cycle (Jones, 1984; Hupe, 2007) beginning with agenda-setting and ending with evaluation and feedback as a frame for understanding policy. There have also been several approaches to policy grounded on bounded rationality and the constraints imposed on decision-making by the absence of full information (Zaharadias, 1999, 2007).

Still other approaches are based on the manner in which the public agenda is determined (Baumgartner and Jones, 2010). And even more approaches focus on characteristics of policy itself (Hood and Margetts, 2007; Peters, forthcoming).

The various approaches to public policy, in political science and across the variety of other disciplines, provide a number of insights into public policy. However, to be able to link all these perspectives requires some more encompassing framework of perspective. I will be attempting to make the linkages in policy through a design perspective (see Linder and Peters, 1984; Schneider and Ingram, 1988; Howlett and Lejano, 2013). Like engineering or architecture, good policy analysis involves bringing together a series of components and processes into a designed intervention into the economy and society.

The political process and the complexity of the targets of policy may make such well-designed interventions more difficult to achieve than for engineering or architecture. Unlike metal or concrete, citizens have minds of their own and therefore making policy depends upon the extent to which citizens behave as expected. That said, however, for the analyst thinking about what a good design would be enables him or her to at least begin with strategies for intervention. That design may have to be more contingent than those in other fields but a clear design is perhaps the best way to begin the intervention.

The fundamental argument of this book is that we can understand public policy through a design perspective, and also that we should consider the appropriateness of policy interventions through a design perspective. The argument for a design perspective on public policy is that there needs to be some clear connection between the assumed causes of the problem being addressed, the instruments used to attempt to remedy that situation and an understanding of what a desirable outcome would be. A design perspective on policy emphasizes those multiple linkages as well as the need to consider policy interventions in a more holistic manner than is generally characteristic of policy analysis.

Saying that a policymaker or an analyst wishes to utilize a design perspective on policy, however, is only the beginning of addressing the issue. The participants in the process must then elaborate exactly what is meant by that design. On the one hand, designing could be considered from a positivist, "scientific" foundation. In such a perspective the nature of the problem to be solved is taken largely as a given, and then various forms of evidence and analysis are brought to bear on the problem to produce a "solution". This can be seen as a form of "normal science" in which the analytics are conducted within a largely agreed upon paradigm.

This scientific approach remains the modal form of addressing public policy problems. Simply because so much policymaking is done within specific policy domains for which the nature of the problem and the range of possible solutions have been well defined. Organizations within the public sector, as well as their clienteles, generally have been able to create some agreement within their own policy domains, so that decisions being made are largely at the margin, rather than about fundamental policy issues. While these "silos" may generate real problems for considering how to resolve larger policy issues they do provide the participants with some predictability and some control over their own policy domains. Likewise, policymakers and their analysts are primarily in the business of solving particular problems rather than thinking about the more intellectual foundations of policy analysis.

Another strand of the political science literature on policymaking and policy design has dealt with this issue of design primarily through considering the ideas informing a design, and to some extent through the framing of possible policy interventions (see Stone, 1997; Chong and Druckmann, 2007). In this analytic perspective policies, and the problems that they are meant to resolve, are primarily social constructions rather than "scientific" in the positivist sense of that term. Giandomenico Majone (2002b), for example, expressed his discontent with the more scientific approaches to regulatory policy in Europe and stressed the desirability of using rhetorical and legal methods for understanding and shaping policy.

Therefore, in this constructivist view, policy designs are shaped through argumentation rather than a rational analytic process (Fischer and Gottweiss, 2012). Rather than having a single answer to the policy problem different sets of argument ideas will be associated with different designs, and may produce different types of interventions. Further, the problem itself may not be taken as a given and will be subject to interpretation – indeed defining the policy problem may be the most important aspect of the entire process, given that once it is defined and understood in a particular way then the remainder of the analysis proceeds from that perspective.

This constructivist conception of design argues that a particular set of ideas define the policy design. In addition, those policy designs can be generated by picking ideas from other settings, defined geographically or through policy domains (Schneider and Ingram, 1988). This approach to design emphasizes the need for design and the need for comparative analysis, but it does not go far enough in identifying the elements of designs that need to be included, and linked together, to construct an effective policy intervention. Constructivist perspectives on policy design have become very popular among governments in the guise of "evidence-based policymaking" (see Pawson, 2006; Botterill, 2013) but in this version the approach appears to assume that policies may be transferred more easily from one setting to another than may actually be possible.

In addition to those two seemingly opposite approaches described above, Davis Bobrow and John Dryzek (1987) have discussed policy design from various theoretical perspectives in the social sciences and their insights into policy. Whereas the ideas discussed by Stone and others (Fischer and Gottweiss, 2012) pertain to the policy issues themselves and their frames, the approach to design coming from Bobrow and Dryzek is more concerned with the social scientific theories that can be brought to bear in understanding and solving those issues. Bobrow and Dryzek are arguing that major theoretical perspectives on policy each contains an intellectual design that also contains a set of possible solutions. Many social scientists do not consider the policy implications of their theories, but they are certainly present and need to be considered.

Yet another version of policy design stresses implementation and the mix of policies and policy instruments that may be involved in particular policy areas (Howlett and Rayner, 2007; Van Hulst and Yanow, 2014). This perspective makes the important point that policies are rarely acting alone, and many policies and policy instruments may be acting upon the same targets. On the other hand, however, this perspective on policy design is perhaps too narrow because it focuses almost exclusively on implementation and policy instruments rather than on the full range of decision-making that must go into design. Still, the emphasis on designing in the context of crowded policy spaces forces the designer to adopt a more comprehensive vision of policy.

Although it is easy to say that policy design is a useful approach to public policy it is only the beginning of thinking about the process of designing policies. There are alternative approaches to the process, and to policy considered more generally, as well as alternative theoretical perspectives on governing. And there is the political process itself that can place numerous barriers in the way of any would-be designer. What follows is an attempt to understand better what is needed for an adequate design of a policy, and the process of producing such a design.

The design perspective

The design perspective presented in this volume will contain three components. The first is a model of causation. Policies are designed to solve some problem or problems in society, and no policy can be expected to be effective unless it has a clear conception of socio-economic dynamics that are producing the problem to be solved. Further, policy problems themselves need to be understood and conceptualized effectively in order for effective interventions to be designed (see Peters and Hoornbeek, 2005). These policy problems may be thought of as somehow objective and clearly identifiable, but they are subject to, and sometimes the product of, politics and interpretation (Fischer and Gottweiss, 2012).

It is important to understand that there may be no single conception of a policy problem, and therefore no single conception of how to address that problem. For example, what type of problem is the drug problem? Is it a law enforcement issue, or a health issue, or an issue of social dislocation (see Payan, 2006)? This framing of issues is a crucial political process, determining not only the types of intervention to be undertaken but also the actors within the public sector who will gain the budgetary and personnel resources associated with the policy. And, of course, the accuracy of the frame may determine whether the policy problem is actually "solved",[1] and what types of outcome individual citizens may expect.

A model of intervention is the second component of any design framework for public policy. What options are available for the public sector, and its allies in the private sector, to intervene and to alter conditions in the society. Understanding interventions requires something of a strategic or governance approach to policy. That is, to be effective policy-makers have to understand the policy process and the variety of points at which they can intervene. To some extent understanding policy interventions requires adequate understanding of the causal processes described above, so that the policymaker knows which aspects of a policy are most amenable to change.

These points for intervention also may be defined by the stage in the policy process or it may be defined by institutions. For example, in federal systems individuals or organizations must decide which of several possible levels of government they will select as the venue when they attempt to change policies (Benz and Broschek, 2012). And it may be easier to alter outcomes at the implementation stage than at the formal policymaking stages of the policy process (Exworthy and Powell, 2004), given that partisan politics will be less relevant during implementation. Therefore, the would-be policymaker needs to make a number of careful strategic choices that are likely to influence his or her success.

A central element in designing interventions is the selection of policy instruments. Governments have a substantial "tool chest" that they can use to attempt to generate change during the implementation process (Hood and Margetts, 2007; Lascounbes and Le Gales, 2007) and those tools have a number of characteristics that must be understood for effective design. Further, as governments have moved away from command and control instruments toward softer modes of intervention (see Salamon, 2001a) the entire nature of policy instruments, as well as intervention more generally, has to some extent been transformed.

The selection of instruments is not, however, a simple technical process but rather is also political as the instruments themselves create winners and losers just as do the substantive nature of the policies themselves. The shift away from "command and control" instruments toward softer, negotiated forms of intervention, for example, creates a very different dynamic within policymaking that involves numerous stakeholders in the selection of policy. Further, instruments such as SNAP[2] in the United States that builds coalitions across conventional policy areas are likely to be more stable than instruments based more on individual organizations and their clients rather than coalitions.

Finally, understanding policy requires a model of evaluation. What is good policy and what is a good outcome from the intervention of government? This evaluation of policy outcomes involves several sets of criteria. The most commonly applied criteria are economic, and in particular those associated with cost-benefit analysis (Mishan and Quah, 2007). But there are also normative criteria, including political criteria, which should also be used to assess how well the public sector has been performing as it makes its interventions (Boston et al., 2010). These normative criteria rarely provide the neat, quantitative answers provided by the economic assessments, but they are equally important in understanding success and failure in policymaking.

A final point about this design perspective on public policy is that I have been discussing the designs policy by policy, but almost all policies are embedded in complex patterns of cooperation and competition with other policies and organizations. Although I will not emphasize issues of coordination and collaboration in this book (see Peters, 2014a, forthcoming), it is important to remember that these connections do influence the success and failure of any individual policy. And the services delivered to citizens and businesses are sub-optimal because of the failures to integrate the services being provided. Indeed, addressing some issues such as crime may be better done, in the long run, by beginning with programs labeled "social policy" and "economic inequality" than with those labeled "policing" or "crime prevention". The world of public policy is complex and interconnected and taking the linkages into account may be crucial for success.

Design and evolution

The design perspective described above tends to assume that the policy designers, whoever they may be, will create a template for policy that then proceeds through other stages of the policy process. With a plan, whether implicit or explicit, for intervention and then a model of evaluation, a design perspective seeks to put the chosen template for policy into effect. This top-down perspective on policymaking is common among decision-makers within the center of government, but generally appears excessively controlling to actors outside those inner circles.

The more purposive conception can be contrasted with a more evolutionary and adaptive perspective. In that adaptive view any initial design for a policy is, and should be, subject to modification as it is elaborated and implemented (see Browne and Wildavsky, 1984). In this view any design made through a political hierarchy or by planning is likely to require adaptation as it confronts the complexity of the environment. The challenge in such a perspective on policy is maintaining the intentions of the formulators of the policy while attempting to make it perform adequately in the real world.

For some political actors that "drift" of policy during implementation is considered a significant problem. On the one hand, the tendency of bureaucrats to act on their own interpretation about the policy often concerns conservatives who believe that those bureaucratic decisions tend to expand the role of the agencies making the decisions (McCubbins et al., 1989). And even on democratic and legal grounds there are reasons to object to decisions that go beyond the intentions of the legislators who had the constitutional powers to make the decisions (Lane, 1983).

The conflicting ideas about the desirability of evolution and adaptation in policymaking reflect underlying legal, managerial and political conceptions about policy. On the one hand, it is easy to argue that designing policy for once and for all is difficult and perhaps misguided, and that building in more adaptive capacity is important for success. On the other hand, legally there is some imperative to implement the law as enacted. For managers in public administration these different conceptions are reflected in the dual and perhaps competing demands to make something happen and to follow the law.

Rationality, risk and design

This book will stress the creation of designs for public interventions in the society. There are certainly some approaches to public policy that do not appear to match this rationalist perspective, for example, the logic of bounded rationality, incrementalism and the garbage can, and these approaches tend to be dominant in political science. However, even those seemingly unsystematic elements can be integrated into the design framework. Or at a minimum these less structured elements of the policy process can be judged against which the realities of formal design of the policy can be assessed.

Phrased the other way round, the concept of design provides a logic against which the realities of policymaking can be evaluated. Even if the dynamics of policy and the definition of the problems are not as clearly delineated as might be desirable from a rationalist perspective, they must still be understandable within the context of a policy process that will produce some form of design at the end of the process. Risk and bounded rationality are not so random that they cannot be investigated through thinking about more systematic design and analysis of policy and policy processes.

Approaches to policy such as bounded rationality and the garbage can emphasize that uncertainty is always present when governments attempt to intervene in their environments. Indeed, that uncertainty may be increasing as an increasing number of "wicked" problems confront governments (Rittel and Webber, 1973; Peters and Pierre, 2013). A range of emerging issues such as climate change, resource depletion and obesity all involve multiple values, conflicting goals and uncertain causal processes, making addressing policy problems increasingly difficult, and the politics of policy all the more contentious. The political contention and the inherent instability of these problems require maintaining openness in the design of interventions and in the implementation of those interventions.

Any meaningful conception of policy design, therefore, must build in uncertainty and risk. This point has been emphasized by scholars such as Yehezkel Dror (1986) and Boin (2004) but remains less integrated into most studies of public policy than perhaps it should be. It is one thing to argue that the rationality involved in policymaking is inherently bounded, but integrating that understanding of uncertainty into the design of public sector interventions is more difficult. As pointed out in Chapter 4 there are analytic methods of utilizing risk when making decisions about policies, and these methods should be incorporated into the design process.

Finally, any consideration of policy design must include careful consideration of the process that generates the design. Thinking about designing appears to imply a top-down, hierarchical process that minimizes political involvement. In any democratic political system imposition is impossible, there is a complex political and administrative process for formulating and implementing policy. That political process has been increasingly opened to a wider range of political actors so the capacity to control the final outcome has been further weakened (Torfing et al., 2012). Although not hierarchical, and often apparently less than fully rational, this remains a design process. Designing policy does not mean that the idea will come from one source or contain one clear idea, but rather this is more an analytic model to understand what is being generated through the policy process.

The state and its allies

This book will focus on the role of the public sector in making and implementing policy. We are, however, cognizant of the role that non-state actors play in this process. Both market actors and civil society organizations are involved in making and implementing public policies, and this role has been increasing in most industrialized democracies, and to a lesser extent in other countries (Zubriggen, forthcoming). The ideologies of New Public Management (Christensen and Laegreid, 2007) and neo-liberalism more generally have tended to emphasize the use of market mechanisms in policy and administration (see Gingrich, 2011). Alternatively, advocates of collaboration and network governance have emphasized the role of social actors in policy and administration (Hoppe, 2010).

The majority of the ideas to be developed in this book will be as applicable to policymaking with the involvement of non-governmental actors as they will be for policymaking that is more state-centric. The same issues of designing policy must be confronted with or without the direct involvement of non-governmental actors. Some advocates of more collaborative styles of policymaking would argue that the process will produce better policies if all the stakeholders are involved, and/ or if market-style instruments are adopted for implementation. But other analysts would argue that difficult policy choices can be made more readily if they are shielded from outside influences and made by responsible government elites (Fung et al., 2007).

Whether more effective decisions can be made or not, it is likely that contemporary policymaking will involve a wider array of actors than in the past. The political mobilization of more interest groups, the emphasis on openness and transparency in governing and additional legal requirements for involving social actors all lead to the greater involvement of stakeholders in the policy process. Although justified primarily in democratic terms this inclusiveness may not, in fact, include all relevant actors – most importantly the public in general – so that conventional representative democracy continues to have a major role to play in legitimating policy choices and in attempting to include a range of perspectives on good policy.

Contents of the book

The following chapter of this book will address the three components of policy design mentioned above. As already noted the book will emphasize the political dimensions of public policy, although it will certainly attempt to include other elements (especially the role of economic analysis) in public policy. When attempting to understand the nature of policy problems, I will also have to think about those problems in the social and economic context that defines them as policy problems, as well as considering their political aspects.

Although not discussed as a separate component of policy design, decision-making is a pervasive element of policy. The other three components of policy design all involve decision-making and there is an extensive literature on how policies are made. The approaches to policymaking range from very rationalist perspectives to perspectives based on almost random confluence of streams. All these perspectives have some validity but they also have some intellectual and practical difficulties. Chapter 2 will assess these perspectives on decision-making and argue for a more contingent perspective on their use.

The first part of the book will discuss models of causation of policy problems. The first chapter in Part 1 will discuss the political processes involved in framing policy issues and in agenda-setting. These are crucial aspects of initiating the policy process, and include numerous political and social actors in that process. The second chapter will discuss the nature of policy problems themselves, pointing to the various dimensions of these problems that in turn shape the policy process and the possible modes of intervention.

The second part of the volume will discuss approaches to intervention. The first of these two chapters will discuss intervention in strategic terms, including political and governance strategies that establish priorities and must also include assessments of risk. The second chapter within Part 2 will be a detailed examination of policy instruments and the means through which public actors, and their private sector allies, can attempt to alter conditions in the society. Policy instruments are complex entities that require evaluation and careful comparison, and often are used together to produce more effective interventions.

After governments intervene into their societies, they need to assess the consequences of those actions. Therefore, the third part of the book will discuss means of evaluating public policies. Just as there are alternative models of causation so too are there alternative models of evaluation. Economic evaluations of policy – generally cost-benefit and allied forms of analysis – are the most common modes of evaluation. The alternative version of evaluation – using ethical criteria – may give alternative answers about the success or failure of a policy. And in addition to these criteria there is the ongoing political evaluation being undertaken by both citizens and political leaders.

Finally, there will be a short concluding chapter that attempts to integrate the three components of design and considers how they interact in the practice of policymaking and implementation. The conclusion will also discuss the problems raised by a design approach to public policy and what future research will be required to make the approach even more useful for understanding policy and actually designing interventions. The principal emphasis of this book is on creating an academic understanding of public policy, but that academic understanding can also be linked directly to actual attempts to solve policy problems.

NOTES

1   Solving a problem may be an excessively optimistic goal. In reality most policymaking is only amelioration and further, policymaking at one time may address the problem but may also create new problems (Sieber, 1980).

2   Supplemental Nutrition Assistance Program, formerly Food Stamps, supports farmers by ensuring markets as well as the disadvantaged by subsidizing food purchases.

2   Policy problems

In the best of all worlds there would be no social or economic problems that would require the intervention of the public sector. But we do not live in that world, and there are a myriad of problems in society that require intervention. The public sector, and its allies in the private sector, may not always want to intervene in these social conditions – whether for ideological or for practical reasons – but often they are compelled to do so. Public pressure and the very presence of some types of problems may force intervention. To understand policy design we need to understand the problems that are being addressed by public sector action, including very broad questions about market failure and social failure that create those problems.

In the most general sense a policy problem is a condition that some or all citizens (and policymakers) find undesirable. These problems may range from simple issues such as litter in the streets to pensions for elderly citizens through to major foreign policy questions. Some of these policy problems may be addressed through private action – citizens may clean up litter in their own streets. Most of these problems will, however, become a part of the political agenda. And with these problems also come a range of alternative solutions that may or may not be suitable as a means of resolving the issue. This common sense conception of policy problems is the beginning of all steps in making public policy.

This discussion of problems will identify some of the underlying characteristics of policy problems. Most discussions of policy problems tend to describe them according to the functional area within which they occur – agriculture, education, defense and so on. However, there may be as much variance within each of these functional areas as there may be across areas (but see Freeman, 1985). For example, the field labeled education includes everything from pre-schools through to research universities, with markedly different issues, actors and politics. And most important for this discussion there are a number of different policy problems within education that require very different forms of intervention. We therefore need to think about not just the titles we see on government buildings when defining policy problems but also their underlying features.

This chapter will examine policy problems in three different ways. The first is to examine the most fundamental issues in public policy – those that define the need for the public sector to act at all. The second approach to policy problems will be looking at the defining characteristics of the problems that arise in more ordinary policymaking, for example, the characteristics of the stakeholders in the policy domain. And finally, and related closely to the second, I will discuss the concept of "wicked problems" and its importance for policy studies. These problems (see Rittel and Webber, 1973; Levin et al., 2012) are large scale, complex and extremely difficult to solve, but also are becoming more important for governments with the emergence of issues such as climate change, food scarcity and sustainable development.

Why have public policy at all?

The first issue about policy problems is why should the public sector intervene at all in the functioning of the economy and society? This is in part an ideological question, with individuals on the political right arguing that the state is justified in intervening only in exceptional circumstances, while those on the left believe that there are numerous good reasons for action by the public sector (Madrick, 2009; Brook and Watkins, 2010). But this question goes beyond ideologies, and there are good economic and political reasons justifying the role of the public sector in contemporary societies. To some extent these reasons are also viewed through ideological lenses, but there can be more objective analysis that may help to resolve the differences, or at least provide support for different ideological positions.

Market failure

From an economic perspective the fundamental argument for the intervention of the public sector is market failure (Wallis and Dollery, 1999). The neo-classical model of the economy is based on a set of assumptions such as perfect information that often simply do not exist in the real world. Given the absence of those preconditions, markets do not work effectively as assumed, and the public sector may need to intervene to rectify the problems being generated by market failure. Again there may be an ideological discussion over how much market failure is sufficient to justify the intervention of the public sector, but at some level the incapacity of markets to function as expected will invoke the intervention of government.

Public goods constitute a major category of market failures. A public good is a good that, once created, is available to all consumers. Since individuals cannot be excluded from consuming the good, it cannot be priced or marketed. Examples of public goods include clean air, national defense and flood control. Although having some characteristics of public goods, public recreational areas and parks are subject to crowding effects – if we all attempt to use the park none of us is likely to enjoy it very much. If anyone attempts to create public goods and market them, those producers will encounter free riders who will enjoy the good but not pay for it. Therefore, governments and the use of tax money represent the only possible efficient producers of that type of good.

The standard model of the market also assumes that the costs of production are reflected in the selling price of the market, but in many cases this is not true. The most obvious example is pollution. The social costs of pollution – health problems, reduced property values and so on – are not reflected in the market price, and hence products causing that pollution are underpriced (see Dasgupta and Ehrlich, 2013). To rectify that problem governments must either regulate the costs of these externalities or force the producers to pay for them through some mechanisms such as pollution pricing (Sandmo, 2000). There can, however, also be positive externalities but typically the producers of these cannot receive their value. For example, if a hydroelectric dam creates recreational opportunities and increases property values of (now) waterfront property the firm building the dam can rarely appropriate those increased values.

For markets to work effectively there needs to near perfect information. Buyers in particular need to understand what they are buying to be able to make efficient, and safe, choices among products. But the financial scandals following 2008 revealed very clearly that consumers did not have that information about the loans they were buying nor about many investment opportunities being offered to them by the financial sector. Given that sellers have little incentive to provide full information, governments must step in to try to force disclosure (in credit cards, for example) or regulate products for safety purposes.

Although monopolies are generally considered failures in the market, some products are natural monopolies and would be produced inefficiently through a competitive marketplace. For example, it would be inefficient to have two suppliers of water operating in the same area, involving multiple systems of pipes, pumps and so on. It is therefore more efficient to allow one monopoly supplier, whether it be government itself or a regulated private company.[1] This preference for regulated markets is true not only for goods like water where multiple systems of supply would be inefficient but also goods that have very large returns to scale, meaning that very large producers can be more efficient than multiple smaller producers. In the case of natural monopolies or returns to scale the public sector must intervene with regulations on rates and returns to capital to prevent exploitation.

Finally, the economic distribution created by the market tends to be skewed, with income and wealth being concentrated among a relatively small number of individuals. High levels of economic inequality have become largely unacceptable in mixed-economy welfare states, and governments have been using taxing and spending measures to at least build an income floor for citizens who have been less successful in the market. This justification for public sector intervention is, however, more ideologically contentious than the others already mentioned. Further, the existing strategies appear to have been ineffective in most countries, as levels of inequality tend to increase all over the world (Xue, 2012).

Social failures

Failures in society that may necessitate the intervention of the public sector are not so readily classifiable as those in the economy, but they are nonetheless real. Issues such as crime, poverty, family breakdowns, school dropouts and so on may have some economic element but they also have a strong social and cultural component. And the absence of clear categories, such as those in economics, make these issues all the more difficult to address through public sector action. The dynamics of these issues are subject to numerous interpretations and hence become highly politicized.

The politicization of these real or assumed social failures has been most apparent around the issue of poverty. The political right tends to attribute the persistence of poverty to failures of individuals and their family structure, arguing that the disruption in social life and the absence of a work ethic tends to be transmitted from generation to generation and is exacerbated by most social programs (Nowrasteh and Cole, 2014). The political left, on the other hand, argues that poverty and social exclusion are more to do with a poor functioning of the market and the failure of governments to intervene through social policies or economic regulations such as minimum wage laws that would produce a living wage for anyone in work (Bernstein and Parrott, 2014).

The above discussion about market and social failures should not let us forget that there are also governance failures (see Wolf, 1987). While markets fail because of public goods, governance may fail because of private goods when government power is used to the advantage of certain segments of society with public money (see Lowi, 1972). Likewise, the public sector may have "internalities", meaning that public sector actors sometimes make choices that move away from allocative efficiency and therefore impose costs on society. These internalities reflect the unequal distribution of political power and ability of some groups to extract more from the public purse than might be justified on economic or moral grounds.[2] Further, at times governments create un-natural monopolies for themselves that stifle competition in areas such as telecommunications and energy.

Characteristics of policy problems

The above discussion of market failure, social failure and governance failure provides a broad interpretation of the problems motivating policymakers (see Peters, 2014a), but once we move from that very general level to the consideration of individual policy initiatives a number of more specific characteristics of policy problems become important for design. As mentioned, simply thinking in terms of functional labels is inadequate for policy design, given the variance within individual policy domains, and the multiple dimensions that may affect the capacity for policymaking for each problem. Further, keeping proposed policy solutions within the individual silos defined by public organizations and interest groups may reduce the probabilities of finding more than minimally effective solutions.

As well as classifying problems according to their functional categories, policies may also be classified by the particular policy instruments used to address them. This labeling is especially true for regulation, with a number of economic issues being described as "regulatory issues". This classification tends to assume that the only, or at least the most efficient, means of addressing an issue is through command and control regulation. But that is not necessarily the case and some issues, for example, pollution that were once considered regulatory are now addressed regularly through instruments such as taxes and charges (Morag-Levine, 2009). At even more of an extreme, the development of "nudge" and other psychological approaches to policy can produce results without direct interventions (Thalen and Sunstein, 2008). Again, this progression of definitions of policies points to the necessity of considering the basic issues of problems rather than using familiar categories.

Although I can identify a number of important characteristics of policy issues there is no clear theoretical foundation that guides the selection of these dimensions of analysis. The literature on public policy has developed a number of ideas about problems but these have largely been developed inductively (see Peters and Hoornbeek, 2005). However, although there is no unifying theoretical frame these various characteristics of policy problems remain useful for understanding the challenges for government when they seem to intervene. The variations in problems can be related, if only loosely, to the nature of the interventions that governments may find effective.

Boundary spanning problems

Having said that the usual labeling of policy problems is inadequate, one of the more important characteristics of problems is the extent to which they are contained within the usual departmental and functional boundaries. Those boundaries are usually discussed in the functional terms discussed above, but may also include geographical boundaries. With globalization and increasing relevance of multi-level governance, policy problems clearly cut across geographical boundaries (McKibbin, 2007). The boundaries between the public and private sectors are increasingly permeable, and pose another variant of the need to cope with policy problems across boundaries.

Although there are important variations within the functional policy areas, policy problems that can be contained within a single functional area, geographical area or entirely within the public sector are easier to manage than are those that span boundaries (May et al., 2010). Within any functional area a limited number of public organizations and policy ideas may be involved, while if the policy problem can be contained to a single or limited number of geographical areas the political conflict may also be reduced.

While the simplicity of policy management may be enhanced by more constrained policy problems, the opportunities may also be reduced. Boundary spanning problems, whether real or framed as being such, make apparent the possibilities for coordination and synergies among programs (Peters, 2015). That coordination may be horizontal between programs and organizations, or it may be vertical across levels of government, or it may be both, but in any case the overall performance of policymaking may be improved.

Stated somewhat differently, the most important problems in governing cut across the conventional boundaries of policy and geography. Therefore, to the extent that governments, and their counterparts in the private sector, can find ways to cope with cross-cutting problems they are more likely to be successful in addressing the major issues facing citizens. For example, if economic policy is dealt with in the conventional manner through standard monetary and fiscal policy mechanisms, some success can be expected. If, however, this issue is conceptualized as "competitiveness policy" then a range of other possible contributions, for example, education and technological innovation, can be used to address the underlying issue and produce perhaps more dramatic results (see Sum and Jessop, 2013).

Public goods and divisibility

We have discussed the need to create public goods as a general justification for the intervention of the public sector into the economy and society. That said, some particular policy problems require the creation of public goods, while others involve creating private goods (those that allow exclusion and can be provided for some individuals and not for others). The difference between public and private goods helps demonstrate that the same nominal policy area can produce different types of problems. For example, defense is usually discussed as a public good, given that the military apparatus once created tends to defend all citizens. However, defense procurement is more of a private good, with firms and areas of the country competing for contracts that will benefit them. At the extreme, in the United States Congress at times demands that the Department of Defense purchase weapons systems it does not want, simply to keep plants open in the districts of powerful members (Bennett, 2014).

In addition to understanding that some policy problems represent indivisible issues, for example, clean air, the difference between public and private policy problems is important primarily because it may limit the range of instruments that governments can utilize when attempting to solve the problem. Many of the policy instruments available to government (see Chapter 6) depend upon providing benefits or incentives to individuals, but if the problem is indeed indivisible then more collective solutions (usually involving law and public organizations) will be required.

Although in many instances the divisibility of a policy problem is objective, in other cases it may be politically constructed. For the advocate of a particular policy one means of "selling" it politically is to convince decision-makers that the problem is indeed an indivisible problem like a public good. If that characterization is true then the problem can only be addressed effectively through the intervention of the public sector. And individual organizations within the public sector may also attempt to define policy problems as being indivisible public goods so that their particular remedies can be adopted and implemented. For example, social programs may be justified on providing a more peaceful and harmonious society as well as through assisting individuals who need assistance.

Scale

The concept of scale for policy problems is to some extent related to the issue of public goods. The logic of scale is, however, that some problems are inherently large scale and need to be addressed as a whole, or not at all. Issues like building a dam or a bridge across a river are rather simple examples – half a dam or three-quarters of a bridge are useless. A more interesting example may be the eradication of epidemic diseases such as smallpox and polio. The World Health Organization has been attempting to eradicate these diseases totally so that not only would no one become ill with them, there would be no future need for immunizations.[3]

Solving large-scale policy problems represents a challenge to political systems that, like most, tend to function more incrementally. The normative argument for incrementalism, and for bounded rationality in general (Jones, 2001; see also Chapter 3), is that humans tend to lack the capacity to make comprehensive solutions to public problems because those problems are complex and always changing. Therefore, making decisions by "successive limited comparisons" can be argued to be a more rational way to make policy (Lindblom, 1965) than more comprehensive interventions. Policies would be made by taking small steps, considering how well the policy worked, and then adjusting the intervention. But that style of making policy is simply not feasible for large-scale projects (Schulman, 1980), no matter how rational it may be in general.

As well as the normative issues in decision-making raised by large-scale policy problems these problems also pose empirical problems within governments. The multiple veto points (Tsebelis, 2000) that exist in most governments make producing large-scale projects difficult. This problem is more pronounced for presidential systems with numerous independent actors but may be true even for parliamentary systems, and especially coalition governments. The multiple actors involved in making decisions and the multiple interests that must be served tend more toward governance by the lowest common denominator and gradual adaptation rather than making bold decisions about large projects (see Scharpf, 1988).[4]

The problem for large-scale projects may not be so much that decisions cannot be made but rather that coherent decisions may be difficult. If there are multiple actors involved, as there will be in almost any decision, then movements away from the design intended by experts or a political leader may be expected. We focus on design in this volume but design can be easy in principle but is more difficult in political practice. Multiple interests attempt to add their favorite ideas to a project ("goldplating" in defense contracts, for example) or attempt to remove elements for financial or policy reasons. The result may be more diffuse and gradual adjustments to problems, even large-scale policy problems.

Solubility

The concept of scale of problems is closely related to the question of whether indeed a problem can be solved. If the problem is defined as enabling people to drive across a river then building a bridge will solve the problem. If, however, the problem is defined as providing effective transportation for citizens then it may never be solved. The size of the population may increase, requiring more facilities, and making automobiles less desirable as the focus for transportation policy. And technologies for transportation may also change, making some forms of mass transit that could have been unaffordable at one time more feasible, or tele-commuting reducing demand for transportation. And even lifestyles may change, with citizens wanting more services and jobs near their homes so they do not need to drive or take a bus.

Transportation is a policy area in which some issues may appear to be solved, at least for a time, but other areas such as education, health and social policy may have issues that can never really be solved. People will always want to be healthier and happier, so that there will be continuing demands for improving services in these areas. And lack of adequate knowledge about causes of many social problems, or the risk involved in many economic and defense policies, means that these policies are often best conceived as experiments, requiring constant monitoring, and continuous attempts at improvement (see Nelson, 1977).

The inability to solve most policy problems for once and for all, and the continuing attempts to solve those problems, mean that most policy spaces are very crowded. There are layers of attempts on the part of government to provide solutions to issues, sometimes building on previous legislation and sometimes seeking to abolish all trace of the previous legislation (see Mahoney and Thelen, 2010). But attempting to eliminate the efforts of the past may be impossible, given that clients remember the old programs and the organizations implementing the programs also tend to remember the previous programs. While continuing efforts to solve problems may represent, as Dr Johnson said, the triumph of hope over experience they may also tend to produce cynicism and a lack of commitment among clients and employees.

The good news, at least politically, is that policy replacement (Hogwood and Peters, 1983; see also Carter, 2012) is not attempting to make policy on a tabula rasa, but rather is attempting to reform existing policy commitments of the public sector. Once the problem has been addressed, and there are real organizations and real clients, some of the political struggles over getting on the active agenda of government have been resolved. Although the existing organizations and clients may defend the status quo, they may also favor change, seeing all too well the imperfections of the existing programs.

If a problem is indeed solved, and even if it only ameliorates the conditions it was designed to solve, it may then generate new problems and new challenges for policymakers. In most areas of governing we do not have adequate knowledge of the underlying dynamics in the policy area to make as effective diagnoses of the problem as we would like. As Richard Nelson (1977) pointed out with reference to attempts to resolve the problems of the ghetto (racism, social deprivation and so on), many if not most policy interventions involve some degree of experimentation. And likewise, we do not understand our policy instruments sufficiently well to be able to intervene as effectively as we would like.

If I consider my transportation example above some of the impacts of initial policy choices and the difficulties of making interventions become apparent. The experience of road building in the United States and elsewhere (Goodwin and Noland, 2003) has been that once roads are built they attract new traffic and become outmoded almost before they are completed. Likewise, the experience of building roads that facilitated travel into urban areas was that they also facilitated travel out of those urban areas even more, thereby contributing to the decline of inner cities. Therefore, both within the policy area and in other policy areas making policy may generate new and potentially more severe problems.

Complexity

Some policy issues are simply more complex than others (Duit and Galaz, 2010). And the idea of complexity itself needs to be considered carefully[5] in policy terms (Table 2.1) because it has at least two dimensions: technical and political (see Bovens et al., 2000). By technical complexity I mean that the underlying causal processes in the problem are not understood fully, or they involve a number of interactions of individual and social factors. Crime might be an example of a complex problem, given that it is difficult to determine exactly what causes people to become criminals. Some aspects of climate policy would also be technically complex, even more so because the interactions among the variables may be non-linear with small changes in some factors triggering much larger changes.

Political complexity means that there are multiple and conflicting interests involved in the policy domain. These interests may also have fundamentally different ideas about causation or what would be a good outcome of a policy process. This political complexity has been visible in economic policy, for example, when environmentalists clash with

Table 2.1   Types of complexity

		Technical Complexity	
		High	Low
Political Complexity	High	Environmental Policy	Education
	Low	Science Policy	Pensions

economic developers over what the goals of the policy should be. Thus, even if there is basic agreement over the nature of the policy and the causal processes involved there can still be very strong political disagreement about what to do. Also, in economic policy responses to the post-2008 economic crisis there have been fundamental differences between advocates of austerity and those pursuing a more Keynesian approach to economic stimulation (Krugman, 2014). And when that political disagreement is coupled with technical complexity and disagreement the processes of making policy become all the more difficult.

We can see the interaction of political and technical complexity by examining Table 2.1. In this table levels of complexity are classified as simply high and low. While this may simplify the underlying dimensions it is still useful for understanding the policymaking challenges posed by complexity. The simplest possible pattern for policymakers would be to have problems that are both relatively simple technically and politically. These tend to occur in policy areas in which governments have been active for some time and many of the political conflicts have been ameliorated if not solved. In contrast, making policies in domains in which there is both technical and political complexity is extremely challenging, and unlikely to produce highly effective policies.

The other two cells of the table also represent challenges of policymaking. When the technical issues underlying a policy problem are relatively simple and there is still political complexity reaching agreement on policy may be easier than when the technical issues are in doubt. When there is agreement on the logic of cause and effect in a policy area, then the politics in some ways may be more intense, given that there is basic agreement on the nature of the policy. Relatively high levels of agreement on policies associated with technical complexity may be able to produce a more experimental, or evidence-based, style of making policy. While experimentation is an important means of addressing the unknown in public policy, citizens may not appreciate being considered guinea pigs.

Governing and making policy always involves coping with complexity, but some problems and some policies involve more complexity. Table 2.1 points to some aspects of that complexity, but in the extreme governments face so-called wicked problems. These are problems that are sufficiently complex and unstructured that making policy choices is extremely difficult. These problems are sufficiently important for emerging policymaking and governance that I will discuss them separately (see below) as a significant mechanism for understanding contemporary policymaking.

Certainty and risk

Some policy problems are very predictable and involve little inherent risk. School officials can know with some degree of certainty that if a child is born he or she will need to begin school in five or six years, so the school buildings, teachers and chalk had best be ready. Migration in and out of the district may affect the final total of pupils slightly, but there is enough certainty to plan effectively.[6] At the other end of the life cycle, pension managers know with substantial certainty how many people will become eligible for pensions in any given year and can plan accordingly for paying those pensions.

Many, if not most, policy problems do not have that degree of certainty, so policymakers must cope with risk and uncertainty (Dror, 1986).[7] Uncertainty is perhaps clearest in international policy areas in which one set of actors is developing policies knowing that in other countries other policymakers are making contrary decisions. Uncertainty is also apparent in policy areas that are heavily influenced by natural events. For example, the Army Corps of Engineers in the United States builds flood control projects based on estimates of the largest floods that would probably occur every 50 years or 100 years (Army Corps of Engineers, 1996). But sometimes their projects have to contend with the 500-year flood, and may fail – the flooding in New Orleans after Hurricane Katrina is the obvious example. The Corps did its job as it is mandated to, but it had to contend with uncertainty and events that were not parts of the planning.

The characteristic of complexity discussed above is also connected to the presence of risk in a policy problem. Charles Perrow (1984) has famously discussed "normal accidents" as part of contemporary society and contemporary policymaking. His argument was that as we depend upon more and more complex systems such as nuclear power and air traffic control we should expect accidents. Therefore, policymakers need to build these risks into their calculations about creating and regulating those complex systems. And citizens may have to be educated about the possibilities of these accidents so they can make their own calculations, and so that they do not expect miracles from technologies or their governments.

The presence of risk in many policy situations introduces the need to include risk in making choices. One means is to attempt to eliminate risk entirely through mechanisms such as the precautionary principle used by the European Union for issues such as genetically modified organisms (GMOs) (Majone, 2002a). While that approach appears to eliminate risk, it does not because it fails to take into account adequately the possibility that there will be no (or limited) negative effects of GMOs and hence there are potentially large opportunity costs being imposed on European citizens and farmers.

We should think of the decisions being made on GMOs as involving risk, that is, the probability of there being harm, and also expected costs and benefits. In this example we will suppose that the risk of harm from introducing a specific GMO is, say, 10 percent, but the risk of harm produced would be very substantial if indeed the crop is dangerous. On the other hand, if the crop is not dangerous there is a potentially substantial benefit from the higher productivity of the crop. We can put these outcomes together in Table 2.2, and calculate the economic outcomes of the choice. This monetary figure does not, of course, take into account environmental consequences that may be difficult to calculate nor potential benefits such as reducing poverty in poorer countries, which are also difficult to put on the measuring rod of money (see Otsuki et al., 2001). Still this rather utilitarian analysis provides a means of beginning to think about the choice that must be made.

Risk is an objective quality of policy settings, but the perception of risk may be as important or more important than the objective conditions.

Table 2.2 Choices with risk

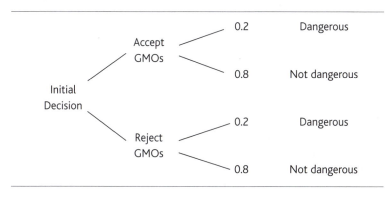

There is an extensive literature pointing to the misperceptions of risk within society (Slovic, 2000; Weber and Stern, 2011). Given these misperceptions, governments may invest heavily in safety in some areas and not in others, or invest more heavily in some diseases than in others even though objectively the relative risk of death or injury does not warrant that distribution of funds.[8] We as analysts may be able to say rather facilely that the perceptions of risk are irrelevant for making real policy, but in the political world dismissing public opinions is not so easy.

Tragic choices

Governments must make a number of extremely difficult choices. The most difficult of these policy problems have been classified as "tragic choices" (Calabrese and Bobbitt, 1978; Brown, 2007), meaning that making choices to benefit one group in the society will inevitably produce deprivations, and often quite severe deprivations, for other members of the society. In its original development, the concept of tragic choices was used to describe decisions being made in the allocation of scarce life-saving technologies, when giving one person access to that technology inevitably meant that someone else would not receive the treatment and would die.

To some extent all choices being made in the public sector are tragic, given that any decision to benefit one group involves deprivations to others, but the idea of tragic stresses that some policy decisions may mean that some people die. So, deciding how to allocate livers or hearts for transplants means that some people will survive and some will not.

But deciding to allocate money to highways or to other purposes may also mean that some people will be saved and others may not. Are the rules for making these allocations fair? And are there a range of cultural definitions of fairness that differ across countries and that may produce different outcomes for citizens?

Monetization

Finally, some policy problems are fundamentally about money and can be expressed in terms of the need to redistribute money. Many common policy programs depend upon monetizing the problems involved. Subsidies to farmers, loans to university students, pensions of the elderly and flood insurance for homeowners all assume that money is sufficient to address, and perhaps even solve, the policy problem. And generally this assumption of the underlying monetary nature of the problem is correct and money is sufficient.

If a problem can be addressed with money then government should consider themselves fortunate. Given that governments have large budgets and have access to printing presses, they can generally marshal financial resources to address a problem.[9] If, however, the problem is based on the deprivation of status, respect and on injustices then attempting to redress those grievances through money would be ineffective and even insulting. For example, some groups have advocated reparations for African-Americans whose ancestors were brought to the United States as slaves (Posner and Vermeule, 2003). While that money might be welcome, it could not adequately address issues of race and deprivation that persist.

When we begin to discuss policy instruments, it becomes apparent that relatively few instruments are clearly connected to altering problems defined by status or respect. Nodality, or information, is the most obvious mechanism for approaching non-monetary problems. But this category of instrument tends to be less directly effective in producing change than other mechanisms such as those utilizing money (treasure) or authority (law). These nodality-based instruments have become more popular as government resources wane and citizens become more resistant to authority (Thalen and Sunstein, 2008), but they generally lack the effectiveness of more intrusive forms of intervention.

Summary

This list of characteristics of policy problems is useful for understanding the nature of the tasks confronting the public sector. Each of the categories is useful for understanding the problems, but there is as yet no weighting of the relevance of each, nor how to link them together to create more complex understandings of the challenges to policymaking. With these characteristics, however, we can demonstrate the internal variations of a functional policy area such as health (see Table 2.2).

These problems, and the understanding of the challenges they present, will serve as the background for other aspects of the process of policy design. If designers understand the nature of the challenges they face they will be better able to understand how to create programs that have a greater probability of success. Further, differences among the nature of problems will affect the policy process itself. For example, more politically complex problems (almost by definition) tend to involve a wider array of social interests, while technically complex problems tend to exclude interests unless they are members of specific epistemic communities. The real political fun begins for problems that are both technically and politically complex.

Unstructured and wicked problems

The discussion above has been based on a fundamental assumption that the policy problems we are contending with can be defined readily and have an identifiable structure. Such problems are the foundation of most policy analysis, given that they can be readily understood and offer some hope of being resolved. Also, policy analysts and policymakers tend to assume that problems are adequately structured and understood so that they can proceed to attempt to resolve them (Hisschemöller and Hoppe, 1995).

The problem for policymakers, as well as for citizens, is that many problems do not come neatly structured. Further, problem structuring is a political process in which individuals with different conceptions of the problem attempt to create a conceptual structure of the problem that can be used to make policy, if not necessarily solve the problem (Dery, 2000). Without such a structure, or in the terms of this chapter some understanding of the characteristics of the problem, policymakers will not be able to address the issues involved effectively.

We will discuss the political process involved in framing and structuring problems in Chapter 3, but here it is important to consider the underlying nature of unstructured problems, and particularly an extreme version of these – wicked problems. Understanding these difficult problems appears to be becoming increasingly significant for governments, as the real world is forcing more of these problems – climate change, obesity, substance abuse – into the public sector, and citizens are expecting some form of public action. These wicked problems are often the most dangerous issues facing citizens and societies as a whole and hence demand some form of public intervention. That intervention may at times be only symbolic as governments have no real answers, but there must still be some response.

Rittel and Webber (1973) coined the concept "wicked problems" to describe very difficult problems facing the public sector. Although originally expressed in terms of planning theory, this concept appears extremely relevant for more general studies of public policy. Rittel and Webber discussed the concept of wicked problems in relatively abstract terms, but phrased in somewhat more operational terms there are several criteria that can be used to characterize wicked problems:

1. Wicked problems are difficult to define. It is not easy to say just what the problem is.
2. The problems are multi-causal and have many interconnections.
3. Therefore, wicked problems are often unstable, with small changes in one possible cause producing large-scale effects.
4. These problems have no clear solution, and perhaps not even a set of possible solutions.
5. Because the solutions are unclear, any intervention may have unforeseen consequences.
6. Wicked problems involve multiple actors and are socially complex.

This characterization of policy problems appears relatively similar to some of the aspects of complexity already mentioned, but tends to emphasize the difficulties in even defining the problem in operational terms. Also, recent research on complexity in public policy (Duit and Galaz, 2010; see also Termeer et al., 2010) has extended the consideration of complexity in ways somewhat similar to the conception of wicked problems. That said, Rittel and Webber appeared more interested in understanding the nature of the underlying problems, while the complexity scholars appear more concerned about the possibilities of solutions.

If wicked problems were not difficult enough, some scholars have argued for the emergence of "super wicked" problems. These problems have all the properties of wicked problems, but in addition have four additional characteristics that confound policymaking even more. These four characteristics are:

1. Time is running out.
2. There is no central authority, or only a weak central authority, to manage the problem.
3. The same actors causing the problem seem to solve it.
4. The future is discounted radically so that contemporary solutions become less valuable.

The concern with "super wicked" problems is obviously closely connected to contemporary questions such as climate change and resource depletion (see Levin et al., 2010), but may also apply to other issues, especially those that have a strong international component. At the time that Rittel and Webber were writing the major empirical referents for wicked problems were urban and social problems, while in the twenty-first century the major referents are global environmental and economic issues. These problems produce severe disadvantages (even when compared with "normal" wicked problems) for society, and because of their global nature also lack a sovereign that can make decisions that may be able to solve, or at least ameliorate, the problem.

Some common issues in defining problems

For all types of policy problems there are some common questions that must be considered in the design of responses (see Weimer, 1993). In addition to attempting to understand causation and frame the problem in terms of causation (see Chapter 3) the problem must be understood in terms of the manipulable variables that are contained within it. No matter if the problem is large scale or small scale, or simple or complex, anyone thinking of intervening must understand what variables can be used to produce change and which cannot. And designers will always be looking for those variables that are the easiest, and least costly, to manipulate.

Another important, and forward-looking, element of problem definition is to consider what the policy area is meant to look like after government has acted? These goals will be different for each policy problem but there needs to be some sense of what the intervention will produce. If there is a problem, then what will be required to eliminate, or at least ameliorate, the problem? As noted at the beginning of the chapter, the common sense notion of policy problems may initiate the process and some common sense of remedy also motivates the process. But that common sense may not be adequate for producing a more enduring design for addressing the problem.

Coordination as a policy problem

Finally, we have been tending to consider the nature of policy problems one by one, but as mentioned in Chapter 1, coordination among the numerous policies within the public sector represents a significant policy problem in itself. Although the coordination problem tends to arise after governments have acted, we can conceptualize this as a fundamental policy problem. As already noted, most policies depend at least in part on other policies to be effective. This interdependence is perhaps most evident in social policy areas (Challis, 1988). Education cannot be effective if students are hungry, or come from troubled homes. And health policies cannot be effective if the population is poorly housed and poorly fed.

As a policy problem coordination has some of the same characteristics used to describe other policy problems. For example, coordination has some elements of a large-scale problem, given that reaching some agreement among the actors involved is more effective if all relevant actors are involved. Further, coordination tends to have a great deal of political complexity. In this case, the political actors are primarily organizations within government itself, rather than external political actors. Each of these organizations is attempting to use the coordination situation as a mechanism for enhancing its own success, as well as to advance a particular policy agenda.[10] Finally, there are interesting questions about what is the purpose of the coordination and how many actors need to be involved in order for the coordination to be effective.

This recognition of coordination as a policy problem in itself (see also Peters, 2015) helps to emphasize the interconnections existing within the public sector as it acts to make policy. We should attempt to understand the nature of the individual public problems and provide some (hopeful) solution for them, but that may only be the start. That action cannot be undertaken effectively without some understanding of the already crowded policy space of the intervention. In addition to the horizontal coordination with other programs, there will also be vertical coordination within the multi-level governance operating in any government system. To some extent we must consider policies one by one, but we must not lose sight of the multiple connections with other policies and actors.

Summary

Policymaking is directed at solving problems that confront the society and economy. Ordinary citizens can identify most of the problems facing them, although they may not recognize all the complexities involved. These common sense definitions of problems are useful but they may not be capable of moving the solution of the problems very far forward. Likewise government organizations tend to think of policy problems in terms of their own interests and their policy priorities. Resolving these policy problems will require more thorough analysis and a good deal of politics, as well as a clear analytic conception of the problems themselves.

Although both academic and popular discourse tends to link problems with particular substantive policy areas, or with particular policy instruments, the reality of policy problems is more complex. This chapter has raised a number of points about policy problems and how their underlying features can affect the types of policy choices made, as well as the success of those policy choices. This discussion of policy problems has been rather analytic, but the next chapter will examine more about the politics of policy problems. This chapter will focus on the framing of policy problems and on how those issues become parts of the public agenda. Our rather academic perspective on the policy problems presented in this chapter will have to be tempered by the political process of framing and defining public sector agendas.

NOTES

1 Historically telephones were also considered natural monopolies but technological change has made the market for cell telephony competitive, if still to some extent regulated to prevent collusion in a market in which the entry costs are very high.

2 A good recent example would be the decision by the US House of Representatives to pass a farm bill providing billions of dollars in subsidies to farmers, most of which goes to very affluent farmers and to "agribusiness". The same bill terminated the food stamp program, the benefits of which go primarily to the working poor.

3 This apparently has been achieved with smallpox (Fenner et al., 1999), and children are now no longer routinely vaccinated. Although complete eradication may be the final goal, reducing the population susceptible to the disease has the effect of "herd immunity", making spread of a disease more difficult.

4 There are some significant exceptions to this rule. More authoritarian regimes certainly can produce large-scale governance, as the success of some of China's many development projects demonstrates. Also crisis, and large-scale failure, may induce investment in large governance projects.

5 And complexity is different from complicated. A complicated problem may have a number of moving parts but the interactions among those parts may be readily understandable.

6 This certainty depends in part on the policymakers having basic information about population movements. However, in many developing countries there may be little accurate information on total births and deaths, much less on the residence of the children being born, so that planning becomes an even more difficult task (UNICEF, 2005).

7 See Chapter 8 on risk-benefit analysis.

8 Approximately 20 percent more people die of colorectal cancer in the United States each year than they do from breast cancer, but funding for breast cancer research is more than twice as high.

9 There are, of course, some real constraints on the capacity of governments to tax and to print money. The experiences of countries such as Italy, Spain and Greece after the fiscal crisis of 2008 demonstrate that those limits on public finance are very real.

10 In this way coordination (and several other policy problems) resemble Graham Allison's concept (Allison and Zelikow, 1999) of bureaucratic politics, in which a decision situation (no matter how much of a genuine crisis it may be) becomes a locus for pursuing organizational interests.

PART I

Making decisions about policy

3 Models of policymaking

The logic of designing public policies is to make decisions about policies that are then translated into action. Therefore, I need to discuss the range of models of decision-making for public policy and assess their utility for understanding how the public sector, along with its allies, function to make those decisions. The literature on public policy contains a number of theories, models and frameworks for policymaking (see Petridou, 2014). Although making different claims about generalization and explanation, each of these schemes argues that their particular perspective provides a useful, if not superior, intellectual foundation for understanding and explaining how decisions about policy are made.

As well as having aspirations of being explanatory, most of these models are also at least implicitly normative. That is, they are arguing not only this is how decisions are made but also how decisions should be made. The normative stance of several of these models of decision-making is not explicit, but there is some sense even in those cases that if the logic of the approach were followed then governments would be able to make better decisions. In none of these models of decision-making can there be a guarantee of good decisions, given that the information and assumptions going into the process may be faulty. The proponents of the models argue, however, that at least the process itself, and the assumptions about how to reach good policy decisions, will not be an impediment to good policy.

Although each of the models of policymaking discussed here has its own distinctive questions and answers, there appear to be two broad sets of approaches. One is concerned with the ability of policymaking to be rational in any meaningful sense of the term. The possibility of synoptic rationality is one of the oldest questions in policy studies (Lerner and Lasswell, 1951, pp. 4–6), and continues to motivate discussions in the field, and most models of policymaking make less demanding assumptions about the process. That said, some form of utilitarian and rational perspective persists, and even dominates, in evaluative models of policy (see Chapter 8) if nowhere else.

Associated with the question of the possibilities of rationality in decision-making is whether decisions are made best in a comprehensively rational manner or whether they should be "good enough" for the short term, with decision-making being conceptualized as more continuous. As well as the capacity to act rationally, this issue is concerned with the availability of adequate information to make those comprehensive, long-term decisions. Are decision-makers capable of marshaling enough information to be able to predict the future state of the policy domain, and to understand all the potential policy options?

The second set of questions about policymaking addresses the extent and the manner in which politics is involved in making policy decisions. As we are dealing with public policy then the public sector is inherently one component of the decision-making, but the question is how are government and politics involved. This question includes the extent to which the formal institutions of government dominate policymaking, and conversely the extent to which interest groups and other social actors influence the process directly. Further, we need to consider the extent to which expertise rather than politics is dominant in the decision-making.

Although it is at a different level of generality, the policymaking literature also raises the question of the extent to which the process itself shapes the policy outcomes produced. Much of the political science literature on public policy emphasizes the process by which policy is made, and tends to emphasize the position and role of particular political institutions in that process (Hupe, 2007). Other models of policymaking are less concerned with process and institutions but rather focus on decisions per se, assuming that the same logic would apply regardless of the nature of the institutions involved.[1]

This difference in emphasis on institutions and processes does not mean that the fundamental emphases cannot be combined. For example, we may consider how rational actors approach function within institutions by considering institutions as collections of veto points and veto players through which decisions must be processed in order to make decisions (Tsebelis, 2000; but see Ganghof, 2003). We would expect that institutions with more decision points would make any comprehensive version of rationality more difficult, with the boundedness of that rationality (see below) becoming more evident.[2] For example, presidential policymaking systems such as the United States with multiple actors and multiple veto players are characterized by difficulties in making clearly defined policy design.

Although this chapter is entitled "Models of policymaking" other important models are located in other chapters. Most notably, the discussion of the punctuated equilibrium model, one of the more commonly used models in political science, is located in the chapter on agendas (Chapter 4). This splitting of major approaches to policy reflects the difficulties of writing about public policies, both in a practical and an academic sense. Although to some degree issues about the individual components of policy and the policy process can be treated separately, in other ways they are intimately connected with the remainder of the policymaking.

Approaches to decision-making and their relationship to policymaking

When we discuss policymaking and policy design we are ultimately talking about decision-making. Having said that, we need to place decision-making at the center of a study of public policy and we must now proceed to discuss how we understand the processes through which decisions are made, and the manner in which individual decisions are linked across the governing process. The models we will discuss come primarily from political science and public administration, and are inherently about making policy decisions. Saying we need to focus on decisions, however, brings forward a wide range of models and frameworks that do attempt to help the scholar and the practitioner understand decisions.

Rationality

For contemporary political science the usual manner in which to begin considering the process of making decisions about governing would be to think of these as a rational process in which the actors involved attempted to maximize their personal or organizational utility. That rational perspective can be developed either in a rather simple descriptive sense or in a more formal manner. In either version of rationality there are a set of assumptions that are fundamental to the approach and which at once strengthen the analysis produced and place constraints on the range of decisions that may be taken.

For our purposes the first and perhaps most difficult of these assumptions is that the actors making decisions have a known order of preferences, and these preferences are transitive. That is, if a decision-maker prefers A to B and prefers B to C then he or she will prefer A to C. This appears to be a rather simple condition for ordering preferences but in complex political and strategic governance situations this condition may not necessarily hold. The potential lack of transitivity is in part because governance decisions involve multiple dimensions so that having to choose A or B or C involves actually making choices about a number of factors – goals, instruments, budgets – that may not all vary together in the preferences of a decision-maker.

A second assumption about rationality in public policymaking is that all the actors involved will have the same array of preferences, or at least that their preferences will be based on roughly similar foundations. Beyond the simple idea that all actors are utility maximizers, that assumption may be difficult to maintain. Policymaking involves a range of actors, all of whom may want different things out of governing, and they may not even be thinking about the same factors. The leader of a bureaucratic agency may be thinking about maximizing the prestige or budget of the organization while the political leader may be thinking about re-election, controlling public expenditure or even the best way of serving the public. These conflicting rationalities then need to be integrated in some ways through the processes of governing (see below). Further, the preferences of the actors involved should be transitive. That is, if an actor prefers A to B, and also prefers B to C, then he or she should prefer A to C. In policymaking that assumption is often violated because of ideological or strategic reasons. If that assumption is violated then making decisions becomes more difficult, especially when multiple individuals with seemingly unstable preferences are involved.

A third assumption about rationality is that the actors involved have perfect information so that they can make rational choices among the available alternatives. And indeed there is an assumption that the actors are aware of all the options so that they can make the appropriate choices among them. In the real world of policymaking there is generally very incomplete information and incomplete understanding of the options (or even of the nature of the problems themselves, see Chapter 2). Thus, given these problems in information, among others, the possibilities for making fully rational decisions is limited, even if the actors involved are attempting to be as comprehensive as possible in their analysis.

Fourth, this model of decision-making would assume that the outcomes of a process can be assessed on a common utilitarian scale of benefits and costs. In the world of politics and governing, however, process may count as much as substance, and image may trump reality. In the terms of March and Olsen (1989), the "logic of appropriateness" may be at least as important as the "logic of consequentiality" in understanding of how to evaluate decisions made in governance. That is, decisions should be evaluated in terms of their normative content as well as their costs and benefits. If this is the case then decision-making about public policy may involve a set of incommensurable dimensions of evaluation, which renders making a reasonable decision difficult.

Finally, a rational model of decision-making for governance would assume that the consequences of the choices being made are predictable and reasonably stable. Unfortunately for policymaking and governance making predictions about outcomes is difficult. There is, for example, a large and interesting literature on the unintended consequences of decisions made in governance, as well as on the massive failures of programs and policies (Sieber, 1980; Bovens and 't Hart, 1996). Thus, even if we were able to provide unambiguous rankings of preferences for outcomes the ability to link outcomes with specific governance choices may be limited.

While the assumptions about rationality discussed above give some cause for concern about this approach to understanding decision-making for governance, we can still gain some useful insights by acting as if the assumptions could be sustained and then looking at the ways in which decisions are being made. The simplest of these ways of understanding choices are relatively simple utilitarian models of choice and evaluation. For example, cost-benefit analysis and risk-benefit analysis assume that the consequences of public policies can be assessed on a common measuring rod of money and that more is better.

It is important to notice in these discussions of decision-making from a rational perspective that the emphasis tends to be on single decisions rather than on the complex chains of decisions that are inherent in governance. Likewise, the emphasis is on a decision-maker or a limited number of decision-makers who make bargains. These bargains tend to be conceptualized as one time deals based on a particular set of preferences. Governance, on the other hand, is a continuous process so that reducing transaction costs among the participants may be as important for the success or failure of the process as the rationality of any particular choice (Stigler, 1972).

One of the most familiar examples of rationality in the literature on governance is Graham Allison's study of decision-making in the Cuban Missile Crisis (Allison and Zelikow, 1999). He examined the behavior of American and Soviet decision-makers during the crisis using three alternative frames, one of which was comprehensive rationality. The version of rationality used by Allison was, however, rather informal and the conditions that would underpin that approach to governing were not fully specified. This crisis also contained multiple individual choices, involving tacit bargaining between the two sides. Similarly, Yehezkel Dror (1986) examined the rationality of decision-making under conditions of adversity in governance, and attempted to understand how governments could make rational choices when faced with a complex international environment.

A more detailed set of models about the application of rationality to governance decision-making can be drawn from the literature on decision science, seeking to quantify the payoffs of making choices under risk. For example, what should a decision-maker do when faced with an event (the landfall of a hurricane) that is to some extent uncertain? There are costs and benefits associated with any action (evacuation or sit tight) and therefore we can consider the likely costs of any action given different sets of probabilities. The typical cost-benefit analysis associated with policy analysis produces the same type of analysis albeit generally without consideration of the probabilities of events.

More formal models of rational decision-making such as game theory contain most of the formal assumptions mentioned above. The individuals are assumed to have a set of preferences to which they can rank and can assign ordinal if not cardinal values. Game theoretic models are largely based on the interaction of two or more actors who may have to make choices in the absence of knowledge of the choices of the other participant(s) in the game. The complex and extended discussions among participants in the policy process do not appear to fit well into these rather restrictive models.

For policymaking these game theoretic models are not particularly valuable because most assume actors with conflicting preferences and the absence of direct bargaining among the participants. The world of public policymaking tends to involve multiple actors with some competing and some compatible goals engaged in long-term interactions with one another over programmatic choices. Where the game theoretic approaches do help for understanding policy is when they are considered over an extended period of time and also involve learning (Axelrod, 2007). In these cases the actors involved learn about each other's preferences and strategies and may be able to produce more cooperative outcomes.

Finally, even if some of the formal conditions for rationality were to be met, a fundamental political question remains about the model. Any strictly rationalist model would tend to depoliticize policymaking, something that may also be virtually impossible in as political an environment as designing and selecting public policies (Elster, 1991). Some functioning policymaking systems such as the Planning, Programming and Budgeting System (PPBS) have attempted to inject greater rationality into the process, but that style of making budgets was criticized because it did not fit well in a political environment.

However, even if rationality is unattainable in reality, does it provide a standard against which to compare the processes and outcomes of policymaking? As studies of implementation (see Chapter 5) have focused on the extent to which outcomes differ from perfect implementation, so too can we learn about policymaking by positing rationality and then seeing where the deviations from that assumption occur. For example, the analytic narratives approach (Bates et al., 1988) used primarily in comparative politics combines a rational actor perspective with case study methodologies to understand how choices are made. The same sort of approach could easily be applied to public policy to understand how choices are being made.

In summary, while we have an ingrained expectation, or at least hope, for rationality in decision-making concerning public policies, producing those rational decisions is difficult. Producing rational action is especially difficult in governance when there are multiple sets of preferences, actors may not even agree on the definition of the decision-situation, and where there is limited and often biased information. Given these barriers to comprehensive rationality, students of governance need to consider alternative models if we are to have a more realistic understanding of the manner in which decisions are made in the public sector, and through the interactions of actors in and outside that public sector.

Bounded rationality

All the problems with a comprehensively rational perspective on decision-making for governance lead rather naturally to consideration of bounded rationality, and means of making decisions that reflect more accurately the complex realities of governance. Indeed, some of the assumptions behind bounded rationality represent marked contrasts to those of comprehensive rationality in making decisions. These assumptions are, of course, also subject to criticism and whereas comprehensively rational models may be too well specified and produce excessively neat answers to governance problems, bounded rationality may provide answers that are too indeterminate and not adequately precise.

Bounded rationality is usually associated with Herbert Simon and his studies of public administration (Simon, 1947). Simon argues that most of the assumptions about decision-making by "economic man" – the perfectly rational decision-maker – are not sustainable in reality. As already noted, in the public sector (or indeed in much of the private sector) preferences may not be transitive, and individuals may not really know their own preference orderings until confronted with specific decision-situations. Preferences in making public policy often emerge based on the feasibility of outcomes rather than more fundamental ideas about the desirability of policies.

Likewise, the information available to decision-makers is far from perfect and indeed if individuals waited for perfect information, or a full array of possible choices in the decision process, Simon argued that they might never make a choice. Given that policymaking is inherently prospective, and that in many policy areas there is not a clear linkage between one or a limited number of causes and the effect being considered, then assuming that one can make comprehensively rational decisions appears more than a little questionable.

The alternative that Simon (1947) proposes to the seemingly severe requirements for economic man is "administrative man". This decision-maker wants to act rationally but also understands that any decisions would inevitably be made within a set of constraints on information and analysis. Therefore the decision-maker is well advised to make smaller, less comprehensive decisions rather than attempt to synoptically rationalize. These decisions should be good enough for the time being – they "satisfice" rather than maximize.

The problem may not be solved but with good fortune it may be ameliorated.

The logic of satisficing is also that the decision is good enough for the time being, and can be revised continually as conditions change, new information becomes available or new actors become involved in the governance process. This version of rationality may therefore be more suitable for governance than the comprehensive rationality described above. Bounded rationality tends to recognize clearly that decision-making is being conducted in a much more complex world than that assumed by many of the rational models of decision-making. Further, it also assumes a more continuous process of making policies in which there can be some learning and some adjustment.

In addition to satisficing as an acceptable, and again desirable, goal for the outcomes of a governance decision-making process, bounded rationality also tends to emphasize routines and standard operating procedures as means of institutionalizing these formats for making decisions. The role of routines within policymaking processes can be seen perhaps better in March and Olsen (1989) on institutions than in the original work by Simon. March and Olsen argue that the logic of appropriateness within organizations involved in governance is defined by a series of factors such as symbols and routines. These routines tend to simplify the decision-making process by establishing bounds on what will be considered, when they will be considered and other factors associated with making the decision. Rather than writing on a tabula rasa, as might be understood from the rational perspective, decision-makers in governance are writing on a slate that is already crowded with policies and organizations, and within which only relatively minor adjustments are likely to be successful.

Although not a product of the same intellectual tradition of bounded rationality, the logic of incrementalism (Hayes, 2006) has many of the same features as bounded rationality. Perhaps most importantly there is the rejection of the possibility, or even desirability, of synoptic decision-making in governance, and with that rejection the acceptance of continuing processes of "partisan mutual adjustment" (Lindblom, 1965) to make decisions. This model of decision-making therefore explicitly accepts that there are multiple perspectives on policy and governance held by multiple actors (the partisan element) and that decision-making in this context is never finite but continuous.

Advocates of bounded rationality and incrementalism will argue that this form of decision-making may in fact be more rational than the synoptic attempts at rationality described above. They argue this position on the basis of two elements affecting decision-making. The first is that comprehensive decision-making may uncover a solution for a governance problem, but it may also fail. When these decisions fail, they tend to fail in a large, visible and expensive manner, which is bad not only in substantive policy terms but also undesirable from a political perspective. If politics is indeed about blame avoidance (Hood, 2011) then making large-scale comprehensive decisions may not be the best approach.[3]

The other way in which incremental solutions may be more rational is that they can minimize decision-making costs. Even attempting to make decisions in a comprehensive manner requires marshaling large quantities of evidence and analysis, and even then it will almost inevitably be inadequate for the complexity of most governance decisions. Therefore, by making a series of smaller decisions, assessing the impacts of those decisions, learning and then adjusting to the evidence better decisions can be made with less investment in the decision-making. The capacity of incremental decision-making to reduce decision costs has been demonstrated most clearly in budgeting, when large numbers of choices involving immense amounts of money are often reduced to simple rules of thumb (Davis et al., 1966). This makes decision-making possible even if those decisions may be less than perfectly rational.

Whether in the lineage of Simon and other members of the school of bounded rationality (see Jones, 2001) or within the incrementalist school, decision-making for governance is being conducted within a set of constraints that tend to privilege certain types of decisions. These bounds are in part cultural, so no American president would think of nationalization as a mechanism for addressing economic policy problems.[4] The boundaries may also be organizational. Governance is conducted primarily by organizational actors and organizations tend to have their own internal logics that they utilize to shape their internal dynamics as well as to present themselves to the outside world (Goodsell, 2011).

The emphasis on organizational actors in governance points to the need to consider the internal dynamics of organizations involved in governance. There is a tendency, especially in the rational models, to consider organizations as unitary actors with a single perspective on policy and governance. That internal integration is not necessarily true either for public sector organizations or for social actors that interact with governments to facilitate governance. Individual members of those organizations may have divergent views (see, for example, the organizational culture literature) that at times intervene in the decision-making.

Thus, there is a need to consider any set of positions taken in a bargaining situation around policy issues to be a temporary equilibrium within the organization and hence subject to change. Indeed, the process of decision-making itself may produce some alteration of perspectives if not of fundamental values. Even if the information being exchanged during bargaining is imperfect it may still be new information that will alter the perspectives of participants in the process, and also reveal new alternatives for action.

Having mentioned Graham Allison's study of the Cuban Missile Crisis above with respect to rational models of the governance process, we can also think of his "Organizational Process" model as to some extent a version of bounded rationality. In this analysis of decision-making the decisions were not structured so much by rational calculation as they were by routines and institutionalized processes. A decision-maker, such as a president, would have to find means of overcoming those institutional routines if he wished to have the policymaking conducted differently. These organizational routines were seen by the participants as means of minimizing costs and of producing predictable responses to situations, whatever that situation may be.

In summary, bounded rationality represents a seemingly more applicable approach to public policymaking than the comprehensive rational model. The bounded rationality approach assumes that decision-making involves actors that are constrained from making any comprehensive decision by the complexity of the situation, the absence of complete information and the routinization of decisions within organizations and established processes. Further, this model is not in any way remorseful over not being able to make comprehensive decisions, but instead posits that ultimately higher quality decisions can be made through this more incremental and bounded process.

I have been singing some hymns of praise to bounded rationality as an approach to decision-making for governance. There are, however, several considerations about the approach that should cause some concerns, both for academics and for practitioners. One is the assumption that decisions can be made again and again, so that any decision made is reversible. While policies are constantly being remade, in the public sector the constraint is that once organizations are created, personnel hired and clients served, remaking the program becomes more difficult than assumed in these models. Indeed, the very logic of routinized and path-dependent decision-making would seem to make continuing replacement of programs very difficult for organizations and managers (but see Mahoney and Thelen, 2010).

Indeed, there is to some extent a paradox in the bounded rationality perspective on decisions. On the one hand, there is the argument that organizations, or other decision-makers, will learn from their own mistakes and adapt. But if their decisions are viewed through the perspective of the bounds of their own culture and values – whether individual or organizational – then they may be resistant to information that does not correspond to their institutionalized conceptions. This difficulty may be evident for initial adoption of programs but becomes more important once initial decisions have been made and with them some understanding of the policy area institutionalized.

Further, the bounded rationality approach may be conservative, and prevent rapid adjustment to changing social and economic conditions. The basic logic of bounded rationality is gradual adjustment of policies to the environment, through trial and error, learning and multiple iterations of policies. That gradual adjustment is suitable for problems that are not severe or which change gradually, but not at all suitable for crises or rapidly changing processes. Therefore, as we will develop below, this model and indeed the others need to be understood and evaluated in context.

Although the bounded rationality perspective on decision-making does assume less structured decision-situations than the rational perspective, it still is not especially well suited to the multiple players and interactive involvement that characterizes much of contemporary governance. Much of the discussion of bounded rationality occurs in the context of a single, and generally governmental, actor whereas any realistic conception of modern governance is that it involves multiple players who may or may not have the same set of intellectual bounds. Social and market actors who may be directly involved in the decisions may well not conceptualize the decision-situation in the same way as other actors involved. These interactions among actors, each with their own bounds and own values, do not fit easily into the seemingly more monolithic model of bounded rationality.

Leaving aside for the moment the practical issues of application of rationality and bounded rationality, there are several analytic questions that arise. Perhaps the most significant of these is the simple question of how big is an increment (Dempster and Wildavsky, 1979)? That is, if we are attempting to understand policymaking, or attempting to advise a policymaker, how large a change can be expected to produce some effects without being so large as to potentially upset existing social and economic arrangements and waste large amounts of resources on a misguided intervention? Unfortunately, the model does not provide any guidance for either the analyst or the policymaker, so we are still left largely with experimentation.

Finally, and to some extent related to the point about the conservatism of the bounded rationality perspective, some problems simply require large-scale interventions. There is a tendency for bounded rationality approaches to disaggregate policy problems and attempt to solve them piecemeal. But large-scale and complex problems need to be addressed more comprehensively, even if the approaches that are adopted may not be comprehensively rational in any useful meaning of that term.

Institutional analysis and development

Although she was a Nobel laureate in economics, Elinor Ostrom was concerned with the range of influences on behavior in making and implementing public policies. Her seminal work on resolving collective action problems (1990) addresses means through which appropriate institutions can overcome problems developing from rational individuals pursuing interests that collectively create social problems. Also, along with Larry Kiser (Kiser and Ostrom, 2000), she developed the institutional analysis and development framework (IAD) that addresses public policymaking in a more general manner, albeit to some extent still colored by concerns with collective action (see Feiock, 2013).

The IAD framework recognizes the significant role that political institutions play in shaping policy, but also recognizes that these structural influences are not the only factors shaping those policy choices. Unlike most institutional approaches this framework is not content with structural explanations but also attempts to integrate greater amounts of individual agency into its explanations. Further, although it has a strong economic foundation it also involves some aspects of the other social sciences as it attempts to integrate individual and institutional levels of analysis. Trust among the actors and institutions involved in making policy is central to the dynamics of the framework (Henry, 2011a).

One of the more important foci for policy analysis utilizing the IAD framework has been the same problems of collective action that much of Ostrom's other work has addressed. In addition to those issues, the framework has been applied to complex governance arrangements such as wilderness management and water systems that may involve multiple actors with different priorities and differing levels of involvement in the process. These socio-ecological systems present numerous challenges to governing, as well as providing numerous opportunities for producing positive outcomes (Ostrom and Basurto, 2011).

Although to some extent based on the bargaining among actors involved in making and implementing policies, the operative element in the IAD framework is a set of rules. These rules exist at three levels – constitutional, collective choice and operational. Further, they may be both formal and informal, moving this model away from the more structured models associated with rationality and rational choice versions of institutions. Thus, this model for making policy stresses the capacity for adaptation and bargaining among the actors, as well as the need to develop understandings among the participants.

Advocates of the IAD framework argue that this approach is more capable of describing interactions in complex, polycentric decision-making environments than other approaches to policy (see House and Araral, 2013. In addition to integrating perhaps the most important of the contributions of the approach is the sensitivity to context and the attempt to develop rules that match particular circumstances. This openness can, of course, also be a problem given the absence of any definitive guidelines or templates for designing policy interventions.

Multiple streams and the garbage can

If we move even further away from the model of comprehensive rationality in governance the logic of multiple streams and the garbage models can provide a perspective that introduces a good deal of randomness in decision-making. Although written from somewhat different perspectives and for different reasons the garbage can model (Cohen et al., 1971) and the multiple streams model (Kingdon, 1985 [2003]) share many of the same assumptions and appear to have relatively common implications for governing. Although discussed as models of decision-making these both (and especially the Kingdon model) also contain significant concerns with the formation of agendas for policymaking.

For both of these models there is an assumption that decision-makers may not so much seek to make decisions as they have decisions thrust upon them. While even in the bounded rationality model there is an assumption (a principle of intended rationality in Simon's terms) that individuals and organizations responsible for governing are engaged in responding to a perceived need to govern a particular domain or to solve a particular policy problem the actors in the multiple streams perspective appear somewhat more passive. They appear to realize that governing is difficult and efforts to intervene in the complex chains of action involved in governing are fraught with dangers for the unwary (see Mucciaroni, 2013). Thus, the most rational action may be avoid making decisions rather than seek to "solve" problems that may not be readily solvable.

Given those difficulties in making choices – the "organized chaos" with which potential decision-makers are faced – the actors in the multiple streams approach tend to wait for a "window of opportunity" to emerge. In these windows of opportunity the several streams hypothesized to be necessary for an effective decision come together. In the garbage can model these various elements of the decision are conceptualized as swimming about in some primeval decisional soup, and when they come together there is the opportunity for decisions, and especially opportunities for decisions that are likely to be successful.

There are several elements that must come together for the decision to be made. The first of these elements is the problem. Clearly both policymaking and governance involve addressing social and economic problems. Whereas for the policymaking models described above these problems are almost inherently prior to the initiation of a decision process, in this model they are initially merely there and become activated as the source of action only when joined with the other elements (see Chapter 2). As we will point out below concerning framing policy issues the problems may not exist for political reasons until they are recognized and conceptualized as problems.

The second of the elements involved in a decision are the solutions. These solutions may be conceptualized as a set of policy instruments (Hood and Margetts, 2007) or as programs integrating resources and law, but in either case these are possible means for solving policy issues.[5] The usual rational logic for policymaking would be that problems pursue solutions, with decision-makers attempting to solve any problem confronting them. In the multiple streams conception, however, solutions may precede problems. Actors in the process may have a favorite solution (a policy instrument), then seek, or uncover by serendipity, new uses for that solution. These solutions can also be seen as means for the organization to enhance its own power and resources within the games of bureaucratic politics (Peters, 2001b).

For governance the third element of this primeval soup may be the most significant for explaining when decisions are actually made. This third element is politics. The problems and the possible solutions can swim around for very long periods of time until the political element aligns with the other two elements. Although these three elements tend to be discussed as relative equals in the decisions, politics create the opportunities for attempting to solve the problem. This activation of the political may be a function of a "focusing event" (Birkland and de Young, 2013), or changes in the governing coalition, or even the result of the charisma of particular leaders (Helms, 2012).

Above we noted that the confluence of the three elements of a decision explains, or at least describes, the timing of decisions. Unless and until the elements come together there is unlikely to be a decision. It is important to note here that this confluence of events is not particularly adept at explaining the content of the decisions. The content of the decision tends to be a function of which problem meets up with which solution in what political context. This random element of the decision process may be extremely unsatisfying for anyone attempting to impose a governance style, or a particular policy design, on a policy area, but in this perspective such "intended rationality" should not be expected to be successful.

As mentioned above, in John Kingdon's conception of the multiple streams approach the confluence of events represented the opening of a "window of opportunity". When these windows opened decisions were possible. This decision need not, however, be made on a conventional ends-means conception of decision-making. Rather, it is equally likely that solutions will chase problems as much as vice versa. For example, we know that organizations and individuals have favorite policy remedies (see Linder and Peters, 1989) and these actors may be looking for problems to which their favorite tools can be applied.

Although the above discussion has appeared to emphasize the passivity of decision-makers in the multiple streams approach, they are also characterized by Kingdon and others as "policy entrepreneurs". The conception that scholars working in this perspective have is that these actors may have ideas about good policy, or good governance, and are merely biding their time until they are likely to be successful in having their ideas adopted and implemented. When the opportunity arises then these entrepreneurs need to be ready to leap through the available windows and push forward with a decision. This description of policy-making actually conforms to the descriptions of many actors involved in government who have ideas on the shelf for years, waiting for the right moment to put those ideas into effect.

The multiple streams approach represents an interesting confluence of possibilities about decisions within itself. On the one hand, there is the underlying assumption that decisions arise when there is a virtually random meeting of various streams required for the decision. On the other hand, at least one version of this approach assigns a significant role for a more activist entrepreneur to help shape the decisions. Indeed, one could conceptualize the availability of an entrepreneur as yet another one of the necessary elements that must come together in order for a decision to be made. And if nothing else that entrepreneur may be crucial to the actual content of a decision, given the policy ideas he or she may have on their shelf, whether central or not in defining the opportunity for that decision.

Political models of policymaking

Differentiating the following set of models as "political" appears to deny the political content of those discussed above. That is not the intention, and there is definitely political content in all the above models of decisions. Rather, the intention of this label is to emphasize the political content of the following set of models, or frameworks, for studying public policy. These models place political and governmental institutions at the center of the analysis and emphasize the ways in which institutions and opportunities for participation affect the choices made. Further, they tend to assume that political values will dominate over economic values in policy choices.

Stages models of policymaking

The stages model of policy analysis (Hupe, 2007; Jann and Weigrich, 2007) has been the mainstay of political science approaches to public policy. The stages model highlights the procedural logic of public decision-making from goal setting to evaluation. This model is primarily descriptive and heuristic, but it also assumes that the passage through the various stages will shape the final policy selected. In particular this model has a certain path dependency with decisions made early in the process limiting the possible choices at later stages. This path dependence may imply some elements of design, although designing policies is not the central concern of the model.

The earliest of the stages models of policymaking was proposed by Harold Lasswell (1956) as a general model of decision-making. He argued that there were seven stages of decision-making, expressed in functional terms, through which decisions must go (Table 3.1). The process began with gathering intelligence and went through to appraisal and termination. In this framework termination was assumed to occur, perhaps because the focus was on individual decisions rather than on programs or policies. Most of the literature on policy termination

Table 3.1   Stages models of policymaking

Lasswell	Jones	Dunn
Intelligence	Agenda-setting	Problem structuring
Recommendation	Formulation	Forecasting
Prescription	Implementation	Recommendation
Invocation	Budgeting	Monitoring
Appraisal	Evaluation	Evaluation
Termination		

Source: Lasswell (1956), Jones (1984) and Dunn (2012).

argues, however, that it is infrequent albeit not so infrequent as the critics of the public sector would assume (see Geva-May, 2004).

The commonly used stages model, rather like that of Lasswell, posits a set of stages necessary to move from the identification of an issue through to evaluation and then feedback (Jones, 1984). This listing of stages does identify a set of important steps in the process, but also begs a number of questions. The most obvious of these questions is that this is meant to be a process, but the emphasis is on a set of stages rather than the process by which these various stages are linked. There is no clear internal logic in the model that explains, or even describes, how issues move from one stage to the next.

In addition, there is no internal logic in the model that explains what happens at each stage, or why it happens. Each stage appears to have its own internal logic and these are not linked by any common theoretical perspective on decision-making. As demonstrated in the other chapters in this volume stages, such as agenda-setting and implementation have their own theoretical perspectives that are largely unrelated to each other or to other aspects of policymaking. Can we make a convincing argument that some other dynamic, for example, bounded rationality, is working within each of the otherwise discrete stages?

Further, the model implies that there is a natural order through which issues will progress. In reality, however, the process may actually begin at almost any stage, and then fill in the missing parts later. For example, difficulties during the implementation of a program may lead to recasting that program and initiating reconsideration. This framework also appears to assume that policymaking is always writing on a tabula rasa, while in reality most policymaking is actually modifying policies, sometimes following on from numerous previous modifications. This continuing modification of policy make some of the stages, agenda-setting, for example, less difficult, but also may make others more difficult.

This simple version of the stages model has been supplemented by other stages models that have somewhat greater theoretical content. For example, Hupe (2007) developed a multiple governance framework that is somewhat analogous to Elinor Ostrom's IAD framework. This model assumes that there are multiple levels of action within government, ranging from higher level constitutional levels to operational levels. The process of making policy therefore involves moving across these levels from grand designs to the actual delivery of the services to the public. This model does the important task linking those levels of action but it also appears to lack agency, meaning that there is no clear identification of the role of individuals in policymaking.

Subsystems: policy causes politics

In addition to the stages model Theodore Lowi's (1964) argument that policy causes politics represents another of the political science mainstays in this area of research, especially in the United States.[6] The more conventional argument would be that political action produces policies. Lowi, however, argued that the nature of the policies would produce different types of political action – regulation, distribution, redistribution and self-regulation[7] as they are processed through the political system. Even if the direction of causation is not always clear, it is clear in this argument that certain political configurations are associated with certain types of policies (Table 3.2).

The two variables defining these patterns of policy are the likelihood of coercion, and how that coercion is applied – directly or through the environment of conduct. For example, regulatory policies tend to be associated with direct controls over individual behavior that are expected to operate quickly. In contrast, distributive policies, such as subsidies, are also expected to influence individuals directly, but to do so more remotely. In all these cases the logic is that attempts to reach certain types of policy goals will necessarily invoke

Table 3.2   Policy causes politics: Lowi

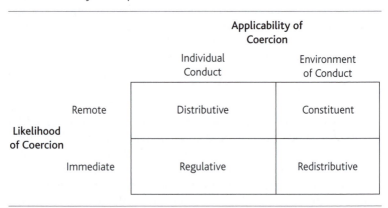

		Applicability of Coercion	
		Individual Conduct	Environment of Conduct
Likelihood of Coercion	Remote	Distributive	Constituent
	Immediate	Regulative	Redistributive

Source: Lowi (1972).

different constellations of political forces and different styles of political action.

The argument that policies cause politics is analogous to some of the discussion of policy problems mentioned below. The need to redistribute income or other resources among groups in society is a particular type of policy problem that in turn requires developing political coalitions of a specific variety. In Lowi's analysis the issue of designing interventions raised by different types of policy are not as significant as the political consequences, but in both perspectives on policy the nature of the policy problems drive policy and political decision-making.

As well as being linked to the analysis of policy problems, the "policy creates politics" logic also has been the foundation of a large literature on policy subsystems (see Freeman and Stevens, 1987; McCool, 1998). The argument for the existence of subsystems has been in part tied to the four policy types that Lowi identified in his initial analysis. And the argument is also more general, arguing that to understand policy we need to understand the numerous subsystems – also called iron triangles, whirlpools and a host of other terms. While we might want to talk about government as a unified entity, this perspective on policy emphasizes the internal divisions.

James Q. Wilson (1980) has developed another understanding of policy subsystems based on the distribution of costs and benefits associated with the policy (Table 3.3). Wilson's argument is that both the benefits and the costs of policy can be either concentrated or diffuse, and those

Table 3.3   Policy causes politics: James Q. Wilson

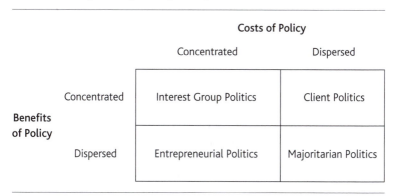

| | | Costs of Policy | |
		Concentrated	Dispersed
Benefits of Policy	Concentrated	Interest Group Politics	Client Politics
	Dispersed	Entrepreneurial Politics	Majoritarian Politics

Source: Wilson (1980).

characteristics will define the type of policy intervention For example, if both the costs and the benefits of a policy are concentrated there tends to a direct political confrontation between the interest groups that would be either the beneficiaries or the payers if the program were adopted.

Lowi's and Wilson's insights into policy were important in activating policy studies in political science, and they continue to generate significant debate (McCool, 1998). While the insights have been influential, they also raise a range of difficult questions. The most important is the direction of causation. For example, if one adopts the multiple streams perspective above, the confluence of the various political actors and conditions may produce a particular policy choice. In addition, the model does not really provide an explanation for the decision process or the decision outcomes. The model does identify an important dimension of policy within the public sector, but does not necessarily provide explanations for policy choices.

The subsystems approach has been extended into an approach referred to as "policy regimes" (May and Jochim, 2013).[8] This perspective also attempts to link policies and politics, and is centered on the policy problem that is the target of policy actions. By beginning with the problem the range of institutional, political and ideational forces that affect the resolution of the issues can be integrated and understood as a collectivity. Despite its attempts to integrate actions addressed at particular problems the regimes approach does concentrate on the role of government actors, tending to ignore the role played by non-governmental actors in most contemporary policymaking.

The advocacy coalition framework

Another political model for decision-making for public policy governance has been described as the "advocacy coalition framework" (ACF). As developed by Jenkins-Smith and Sabatier (1999), this framework addresses policy change more than initial interventions by governments into a policy domain. Further, the ACF model of decision-making is based more on ideas other than the others discussed above. Although the model is based more on policy change than the others, as noted in several places, most policymaking actually involves adjustments to existing policies rather than making policy entirely from scratch. Thus, change may be more of an issue for governance than it might be thought to be.[9]

The fundamental assumption of this ACF model is that there is a set of core ideas that defines a policy. Although there is a core of ideas, these ideas vary in terms of their centrality for the policy (or governance area) in question. An organization or other actor will attempt to protect their core ideas against change, but will be willing to change more derivative ideas at the perimeter of their policy space. This change in policy will come about when the status quo in the policy domain is confronted with a challenge to the programs from some other actor that has ideas that to some extent overlap and to some extent contradict the dominant set of ideas operating within the governance domain.

As implied above, this approach to policy change and governance assumes that subsystems are the dominant arenas for governing (Cook, 2010). Much of governance theory tends to look at whole systems of governing and to make assumptions about them, but the ACF focuses on more tightly defined subsystems, with actors involved having core beliefs that tend to be stable. Thus, there are some similarities with the multiple streams approach in that shifting away from the status quo tends to be difficult. However, unlike the seemingly random nature of the multiple streams perspective governance here is more purposive, and more driven by conflicting ideas than the random confluence of events.

This conception of decision-making may be especially useful for the more interactive versions of governance we are including along with more state-centric conceptions of governance (Torfing et al., 2012). In these cases we would conceive of the social actor – be it market or non-market – as presenting some ideas that challenge the status quo. Although in most cases this status quo will be defined by an actor within the public sector it may also be that the dominant approach to governance is defined by other social actors, or a coalition of public sector and social actors. Whatever the source of the dominant governance arrangements, there will be challenges and those interactions must be understood to understand governance.

The interaction of the dominant governance arrangements and the challenges coming from external actors, whether they are state or non-state actors, in the process of producing a new equilibrium should be conceptualized as a decision-making process. In this perspective on policy, the actors tend to bargain over changes in the status quo, but more importantly they learn about the ideas of the other actors and the potential for constructive change. This conception of decision-making in governance is therefore more open to external influences than many others, and assumes that interactions among actors produce the capacity for improvement in governance.

The advocacy coalition model of decision-making adds to the other approaches discussed here by bringing in the need for bargaining more explicitly. The other approaches appear to have a more hierarchical conception of the manner in which decisions are made, differing primarily in the extent to which rationality, in any comprehensive sense, can be expected to emerge from the process. The ACF assumes that there are at least two possible policy coalitions available, each with a set of beliefs about policy and governance. Through a process of negotiation and learning, a dominant coalition will be able to impose some or all of its wishes on the area. That said, the process through which that bargaining is conducted is not specified as clearly as it might be. Further, the confrontation of different ideas may, however, exacerbate polarization among approaches rather than producing compromise (Henry, 2011b).

Powering, puzzling and so on

The stages models of policymaking address some elements of the political process, but do not address questions about what actors are involved and influential. Understanding the course through which policies are adopted and enacted is important, but identifying the key actors is at least as important While perhaps not as clearly articulated as a theory of policymaking as some of the approaches discussed above, Hugh Heclo's observations about decision-making in pension reform in Britain and Sweden (1974) do point to important issues in making policy. Heclo observed that there were two dominant governmental styles of making policy. One depended upon formal hierarchy, and the associated political power, to make policy decisions and to ensure that they were enforced. The authoritative policymakers involved in policymaking may take advice, but in the end they would be able to make their decisions based primarily on their formal positions in the political system.

The alternative perspective identified by Heclo was characterized as "puzzling", as opposed to powering. In this second approach to making policy decisions information and analysis are more important than the relative power of the actors involved. This puzzling approach assumes that the best ideas will prevail in policy, and that the policy process can be designed to maximize the role of knowledge. While the puzzling approach cannot function without being backed by adequate political power, it will use that power to validate policy choices made by more analytic means.

The initial puzzling and powering dichotomy provided an interesting political perspective on decision-making, but other scholars have added other dimensions to that analysis. Most importantly, Robert Hoppe (2010) added a third component of "participation" to the possible styles of decision-making. This addition reflects the increasing importance of mechanisms for direct public participation in shaping public policies, as well as the established patterns of accommodation in many Northern European countries. That participation is being manifested through networks, deliberative mechanisms or a range of other possibilities.

As well as maintaining the alliteration, the addition of participation to the initial dichotomy reflects different influences on policy than might be manifested through the two other styles of policymaking. Both the puzzling and the powering metaphors imply more elitist styles of decision-making, while adding participation adds more of a populist dimension. Making decisions about policy, especially complex policy issues, may always have a strong elite component but at the same time there are means of involving the public and adding different perspectives to the process.

Pepper Culpepper (2002) added yet another alliterative component to this analysis – "pacting". By this he meant the use of social pacts as a means of institutionalizing the interactions between social actors and the policymaking process. Social pacts (Rhodes, 2001) are analogous to corporatism (Molina and Rhodes, 2002) as a means of formally linking interest groups and other organized interests to the state and to the policy process. Thus, "pacting" is a specialized version of participating, but that participation is more structured than the perspective on participation discussed by Hoppe. Further, pacting adds another source of political power to the process by adding the active involvement of interests potentially affected by the policies.

Finally, Mark Blyth (2007) added "persuading" to this litany of political approaches to policymaking. This addition points out that discussion and persuasion play a major role in the policy process. The "persuading" perspective does not go as far as the argumentative approach discussed earlier (see Chapter 1; see also Stone, 1997) but it does emphasize the use of ideas in debates over policy – and not just the ideas of experts as implied by the "puzzling" perspective but also broader participation through means approaching deliberative democracy. This perspective further can be seen to constitute a general version of the ACF in which the advocacy of different ideas about policy is also central to understanding policy dynamics.

All these words beginning with "P" make several important points about how policy gets made in the political arena. First, as we are talking about public policy, there is a role for political power, but that power often is incapable of being exercised as raw power, especially in a democratic system. Experts, social actors and even the general public may have some things to say about the policy choices being made. Further, these versions of policymaking do not emphasize the policy process to the extent of some other models, but they do assume that process, especially the interactions among numerous actors, is significant in shaping the policy decisions. And finally, these models are all about making decisions as crucial for any understanding of public policy.

Contingent models and choices

We have now identified several important models for policymaking. We have made some allusions to the settings in which one or the other frameworks may be particularly useful, but in this section we want to expand that discussion and attempt to make even closer linkages between policymaking models and environmental considerations. The remainder of our discussion of policymaking models will be focused on the manner in which decisions are made in different policy areas and in different institutional settings.

The examples drawn from the Cuban Missile Crisis point to one important dimension of variation – the extent of real or perceived crisis (see Boin, 2004) – but there are a host of other variables that might be included. Perhaps the most fundamental point here is that policymaking is not the same across policy areas and dependent on the degree of urgency in making a policy choice. As Chapter 4 tends to focus on differences in decision-making across different political systems, this section will place greater attention on the role of particular types of issues, and the role of different types of situations, in shaping governance. This list will not be exhaustive, given the wide variety of influences there may be over governance, but it is intended to provide some insights into the variability of decision-making for governance.

The most fundamental difference among policy issues is the extent to which they are programmed. That is, to what extent are the actors and the premises for decisions well established through law or through institutionalized patterns of interaction. The policy regimes literature with its emphasis on more or less formalized interactions appears particularly well suited to address highly legalistic, programmed decisions. The advocacy coalition approach also appears well suited here, given that it assumes there is an established pattern of policy that is subjected to pressures for change.

For example, neither the causes nor the remedies of so-called "wicked problems" (see Chapter 2) such as poverty or many aspects of environmental policy are well identified. Therefore, rational, and perhaps even bounded rationality, approaches would not be particularly useful for these cases. More politicized and experimental interventions may be the only available options for difficult policymaking situations such as those. Unfortunately, however, governments cannot avoid responsibility for intervening into these difficult issues, so the less formal means of decision-making become crucial.

Conversely, highly programmed decisions may approach the criteria required for rational decision-making. This is perhaps particularly true if the decision is remaking an existing policy for a second, or third, or nth time (see Hogwood and Peters, 1983). In such situations the preferences of the actors should be relatively clear, the consequences of decisions may be more knowable and information sources may be better developed. These conditions may also be seen as reflecting bounded rationality, with the experience of the actors in this particular policy area representing the bounds that can make decisions more feasible.

As mentioned above, crisis also may be the antithesis of programmed decisions. Crises tend to reduce the capacity for rational decision-making given that preferences may not be knowable in a fluid situation and the range of decision premises will not be constrained (Boin et al., 2005). To some extent crises are examples of decision-making through multiple streams, with the crisis being analogous to a window of opportunity in which the demand for decisions may force bringing together solutions with the problem presented by that crisis.

In addition to the nature of the problems being confronted, the political environment of policymaking also affects the relative utility of these frameworks. Frameworks such as the stages models are likely to be more effective in institutionalized political systems. Also, political systems that have greater policy analytic capacity will be capable of governing more by "puzzling" than by "powering". These systems with greater policy capacity, including analytic capacities, also may be able to approach rational policymaking more closely than those without such capacity.

Summary: multiple models, but what is missing?

There is no shortage of models and frameworks directed at making and understanding public policies. Indeed the multiplicity of models makes doing them all justice in this one chapter extremely difficult. The models all provide some insights into these processes, and all offer some explanations for the outcomes of those processes. And they all have weaknesses and blind spots that prevent their being complete and dominant explanations for policy. This combination of strengths and weaknesses in the frameworks leads to at least two significant questions about how to advance the understanding of policymaking.

One means of attempting to address this broad array of approaches, each of which does some things well, but others not so well, is to consider combinations of approaches. For example, the multiple streams perspective on policy describes the almost random elements of some policymaking well, but it tends to be largely institution-free. Can we combine that approach with the stages approach that emphasizes institutions and more formal aspects of government? This marriage of approaches might illuminate not only the processes at each stage of policymaking but also the role that institutions can play in developing and channeling the streams of influence.

These models might also be enhanced by adding yet additional elements to the models. For example, most of these approaches to policy tend to downplay the role of agency. Therefore attempting to include individual-level behaviors into these models should not only help to explain more about the manner in which decisions are made but also remove some of the more mechanistic features of the models. The role of the policy entrepreneur is one example of adding agency to a model that might otherwise depend excessively on randomness.

Further, these models are all discussed in rather generic terms, even if they are largely derived from the experiences of industrialized democracies, and therefore greater understanding of context would also add to the utility of these approaches to public policy. Some of the models may be less applicable in other social, economic and political settings. For example, the ACF appears to depend upon multiple sources of policy ideas that can contend in a relatively open policymaking arena. Both the absence of contending sources of policy ideas, and the closure of possible answers because of ideology or partisan domination, may make this model less relevant in many international settings.

NOTES

1 On this point see the critiques of "decisionism" in public administration and policy studies.

2 This argument is similar to that of Pressman and Wildavsky (1974) concerning implementation, with larger numbers of veto points (clearance points in their terminology) likely to produce failure, or certainly deviations from the intentions of the policymakers. See Chapter 5.

3 But sometimes this is the only viable approach to the issue being confronted (Schulman, 1980). Large-scale issues, as described in Chapter 2, require large-scale and comprehensive solutions.

4 Except, of course, when they do. Both George W. Bush and Barack Obama partially nationalized automobile manufacturers, banks and insurance companies in response to the financial crisis beginning in 2007.

5 Solving may be an excessively optimistic word. Most policy areas, and domains of governance, are never really solved but represent overlays of multiple attempts at solution (Hogwood and Peters, 1983; Carter, 2012).

6 Jeremy Richardson's (1982) ideas about policy styles are not dissimilar from Lowi, and have been more influential in European political science.

7 In another version of the argument, Lowi (1972) replaces "self-regulation" with "constitutive" policies. That latter term means policies designed to shape the formation of other policies.

8 See also the literature on urban regimes (Pierre, 2014).

9 Indeed, the tendency of the literature on governance and policy to write as if decisions were innovations may seriously misrepresent governance.

4 Agendas, agenda-setting and framing

Before the public sector can act on a policy problem it must find a way to move it from a matter of general social concern into the public arena for consideration. There is no shortage of important issues that governments could, and should, act upon, but for governments to make those policies the issue must work its way from some concern in society, or perhaps a negative segment of society, into the institutions of government. That movement on to an active agenda of government requires political action, often by political parties or interest groups. That said, governments are by no means totally passive, waiting for issues to come over their proverbial transoms. Rather, many actors in government, perhaps especially the public bureaucracy, are active in creating their own agendas for collective action.

Issues that do make it to some collective agenda for action are not necessarily successful – they only have an opportunity for action. The absence of guarantees for success is in part a function of how quickly issues move on and off active agendas. This "issue attention cycle" reflects not only the fickle nature of public opinion but also the pressures of numerous issues on governments that have limited time and resources (Downs, 1972). There is always something else occurring in the economy and society that can excite the public, the media and government, and hence any one issue may have a relatively short appearance on the political stage.

This chapter will examine the process of agenda-setting in government. I will first discuss the nature of agendas themselves, and some means of shaping issues so that they have a greater probability of making it on to an agenda. This includes the basic issue of how to frame issues for action in the public sector. I will then conclude the chapter by discussing several theories about agenda-setting and the politics of forming agendas. This chapter will deal very much with the politics of issues and agendas, while the following chapter will discuss issues and policy problems more from the perspective of policy analysis.

Agendas and agenda-setting

I have already made the point that agendas are crucial for making policy, but just what is an agenda. In its simplest form an agenda is the set of all issues that governments (again, along with their allies) will act upon (see Cobb and Elder, 1972). To examine this aspect of the policy process in somewhat greater detail there are at least three forms of policy agendas. The most general version of agendas is the "systemic, or informal, agenda", meaning all those issues that have been accepted on to the agenda for consideration, whether they are actually being actively considered at any one time. The systemic agenda will include a large array of issues that have been accepted as legitimate objects of action by the public sector. Some may be considered settled for the time being, but can be reactivated when change is desired. For example, European governments have a well-developed interest in the welfare state but may not be legislating or adjudicating about it during any one period.

At a second level of generality there are "institutional agendas" that contain the issues that an institution is working on actively at any time. Different institutions may or may not be processing an issue at any one time, and issues may move back and forth among institutions. One important political challenge for agenda-setters, therefore, is to move issues along. The bureaucracy, of course, is almost always processing issues as they implement programs, and the individual administrators tend to develop ideas about how to improve the policies for which they are responsible. Their task, therefore, is to find ways to move those concerns into legislatures or the political executive in order to have the laws changed.

Politically, it is crucial to understand how an issue moves from the informal agenda to some formal institutional agenda. After the initial recognition of the underlying problem in the society, the second stage is that those perhaps vague worries about a social situation have to be specified in a manner suitable for being addressed through the policy process. After that specification of the issues to be considered, concern with the issue must be expanded to include a wider range of political and social actors so that some coalition can be built to enact the desired reforms. After the issue has been made sufficiently broad it can then be moved on to an active agenda in some institution or another.

Different types of political systems provide more or fewer institutional agendas for the would-be agenda-setters. For example, federal and other decentralized systems provide another whole set of institutional opportunities for agenda-setters (Chappell, 2002). Likewise, systems such as the United States and Germany that have powerful and active court systems provide another option, and one that has proved significant in dealing with issues such as civil rights that were difficult to process through the more political institutions (Rose-Ackerman, 1996). That said, multiple points of access for agenda-setters may mean that although access is easier, moving issues around among the institutions and making definitive decisions may be more difficult than in simpler systems.

The availability of multiple points of entry into the policy process provides the participants opportunities for venue-shopping (Baumgartner and Jones, 2010). This search for the institution offering the best opportunities for any particular policy may be highly strategic, but often there is inadequate information to make such choices. Further, different venues may provide opportunities for advocacy groups that go beyond winning or losing on a single issue and open new opportunities for action, and for gaining new partners in their political struggles. In particular the increased internationalization of policies offers new venues with great potential for groups seeing policy change (Pralle, 2003).

Finally, some issues are on "recurrent agendas". The most obvious example is the public budget that in most political systems comes on to the agenda every year (see Walker, 1977). And given that all public programs require budgetary funds, this means that to some extent every program comes on to the agenda regularly, even if the substance of the program may not be debated to any great extent. In addition, many programs are authorized for only a limited period of time, requiring them to come on to the agenda regularly. This recurrence may be beneficial to popular programs but is a threat to less popular programs that may be better served by having issues remaining settled and off the active agenda.

Shaping issues for the agenda

Getting an issue on to any one of these agendas is important for the advocates of a program, but these advocates are often at the mercy of other forces. That said, however, those advocates can attempt to shape issues so that they are more likely to place them on the agenda. Some aspects of issues may not be controllable by their supporters, but others can be. In either case, understanding characteristics of issues that enhance the ease with which they can be placed on to the agenda can inform the strategic choices of advocates, as well as their understanding of the likelihood of success in the process.

Issues are easier to place on to the agenda if their effects are, or are perceived to be, severe. It is easier to place AIDS, Ebola or a severe outbreak of influenza on the political agenda than the common cold, even though many more people are likely to catch colds. And influenza outbreaks may be even easier than AIDS because there is no stigma potentially associated with the disease. Similarly, governments – even the neo-liberal American government – were able to make much more extensive interventions in the economic crisis following 2008 than they might in minor downturns of the economy.

As well as having severe effects, it may be beneficial to the would-be agenda-setter if the effects cover a large number of people. Further, the possibilities of placing an issue on to the agenda are increased if the effects are concentrated, either geographically or socially. For example, higher levels of unemployment are always important politically, but may be more of an issue if that unemployment is concentrated in one area of the country, or in one social group. And that effect may be magnified if the group or region has been the subject of other deprivations, for example, immigrants in most European countries.

The previous two criteria can justify the use of terms such as "emergency" or "crisis" as a means of moving issues on to the agenda. For example, labeling long-term unemployment insurance in the United States as emergency was used as a means of bringing it back on to the agenda for additional consideration and extension in 2014. As we will discuss below, the literature on "focusing events" as a means of explaining agenda-setting also utilizes crisis as a means of explaining how issues can be moved on to an agenda. Even though a policy problem may exist for some time, it will not be addressed until an event brings the problem into sharper focus.

Placing an issue on to the agenda is also facilitated by attaching important political symbols to the issue and to the programs used to address the issue. For example, children are commonly a powerful political symbol, so even programs that may go against the normal political grain of a country can be successful if they can be "sold" as creating benefits for younger citizens. Also, at least in the United States, defense and national security have been important symbols so it is no surprise that the interstate highway system is formally labeled the National Defense Highway System.

One particular version of symbols involved in setting agendas is the availability of analogies of policy situations and policy interventions. The use of analogies is more common in making foreign policy than in making domestic policy (Houghton, 1998), but being able to make a contemporary issue appear like an older issue can be useful politically. If policymakers can say, "We have done this before" or "When something like this happened previously it was a major problem" those policymakers have a better chance to persuade others that they should intervene. The analogies are often false, but they can still be persuasive. And analogies can also be used to prevent action, for example, if it can be argued that when this type of problem was addressed before it proved to be insuperable or that something that appeared to be an impending crisis was really quite minor.

The active political agenda-setter is capable of assisting in getting issues on to the agenda. While some aspects of issues are givens, others can be molded in ways that can make them more likely to be placed on to an active institutional agenda. This activity by interested individuals can be crucial, given the large number of issues that compete for attention by government. This advocacy and shaping of issues is a rather basic way of understanding agenda-setting, but the importance of this stage of policymaking has produced a range of theoretical models of this process. And the possibilities of manipulating issues in ways that can make them more amenable to being placed on to the agenda leads on to a discussion of framing issues.

The politics of agendas

While all the above discussion is to some extent political, we should consider some specifically political models of how issues are developed and then placed on to agendas. The most fundamental issue in understanding the politics of this part of the policy process is the extent to which it is open to popular ideas, as opposed to being controlled by political elites or powerful interest groups. As is so often the case, there is some evidence supporting all these positions and the apparent strength of one or another of the perspectives on agendas may depend upon the policy area being considered or the political system within which the agenda-setting process is being conducted.

The elitist position on agenda-setting is perhaps the easiest to maintain. This argument is simply that political and economic elites dominate the process of setting agendas, as well as politics more generally. Even in political systems that are nominally democratic, or indeed truly democratic, the capacity of money for campaigns, party support or even direct bribery may give the more affluent greater influence. Even if money is not involved, the political and economic elites tend to move in the same social circles, and often come from common backgrounds, so that the elite will have greater opportunities for influence and control. And the elite also may control the media so that the information available for policymakers may also be skewed in certain directions (Carnes, 2013).

The pluralist or more egalitarian position is that democratic systems tend to be open to a variety of influences so that there is roughly equal opportunity for all to influence agendas (McFarland, 2004). In this view the public sector is an open arena within which various interests contend for influence, with no certain winners and no certain losers. Adherents to this position can point to a variety of successes for the interests of less affluent citizens and minority interests. This position appears particularly viable in countries such as Germany, Canada and the United States where multi-level governance and a reasonably activist judicial system provide more opportunities for access than in more confined political systems.[1] Even in more centralized regimes there may be structures that facilitate the influence of non-elite actors.[2]

When we consider agenda-setting and the relative power of different actors to influence the agenda we usually consider the evidence concerning who is successful in getting their issues moved from some broad agenda on to an active institutional agenda, and then in winning once the issue is acted upon in government. We should, however, also examine the capacity of powerful actors to prevent issues from being considered at all. This "second face of power" (Bachrach and Baratz, 1962; see also Lukes, 2004) demonstrates that the most certain way of preventing any threat to the positions of entrenched interests would be to have the concerns of outsiders totally ignored by decision-makers in the public sector.

Another means of classifying the agenda-setting process is to consider whether the impetus for new policies, or for policy change, comes from outside government or from inside. We tend to think of the politics of agenda-setting as involving individuals and groups on the outside of the public sector attempting to press their views on the public sector. While that is certainly true for most policymaking, there are also numerous instances in which government organizations and actors are the prime movers. There is some tendency to consider the bureaucracy as faceless automata without policy ideas of their own, but that is rarely true, and public servants who have been working in a policy area for years will clearly have ideas about how to improve policy.

The agenda items coming from within the public sector may not be major transformations of public policy but there are numerous instances of change, especially reforms of existing programs. The role of actors within the public sector as agenda-setters – usually the public bureaucracy – may be especially relevant within the "multiple streams" approaches to policymaking such as that of Kingdon or the "garbage can" (see Chapter 3). That is, members of the bureaucracy, or organizations with clear policy ideas, may wait for an opening presented by a change in government to bring those ideas forward for action.

Summary

From the above it should be clear that the agenda for policymaking in most instances is made – it does not just happen. Political actors, both inside and outside government, are actively involved in moving issues on to the active agenda of political institutions. Other actors may be working as vigorously to prevent those issues from being considered. That said, however, these actors are to some extent at the mercy of external forces in society that heighten the attention of the public and political elites in certain issues and dampen concern about others. The role of the media in both reflecting and activating attention to policy issues has produced a significant strand of research in public policy, a subject to which we now turn.

The issue attention cycle

One of the more important models of agenda-setting within political science began with a rather simple observation that has been referred to as the "issue attention cycle". Anthony Downs (1972) observed that issues came on to the political agenda with "alarmed discovery" but once the real difficulties of actually doing anything significant and successful about the issue become apparent then the interest tends to wane. Further, concern about most issues is quickly replaced by interest

in the next issue, and then concern about that first issue becomes qui-
escent. That first issue remains part of the systemic agenda, albeit not
an active agenda, until it becomes activated again.

The second root of this strand of literature is E.E. Schattschneider's
(1962) discussion of the expansion of political conflict. His argument
was that the political system in the United States tended (and still
tends) to segment policymaking and to prevent actors not usually
involved in a particular policy domain from breaking through and
influencing choices. This segmentation tends to maintain existing patterns of policy and permit only incremental forms of change. Once
settled, the institutions and the powerful actors who work within them
prevent an issue from being considered by a wider range of actors, or
perhaps all. This is analogous to the arguments of the historical institu-
tionalists (Robinson and Meier, 2006) that policies are path dependent,
with change coming through major events – punctuated equilibrium.
Although this rather pessimistic model of government was developed
in reference to the United States, similar patterns can be observed in
other political systems.

Following from this initial observation a more elaborated version of
this approach has been developed as "punctuated equilibrium theory"
(Baumgartner and Jones, 2010). This is one of several models in the
social sciences that assumes the presence of an equilibrium that is
disturbed by some external force. In terms of setting agendas the presence of an equilibrium means that the policy process can be extremely
conservative. In this perspective issues and particular ways of conceptualizing issues will persist without some sort of exogenous shock, or
perhaps without the presence of a policy entrepreneur.

Information processing plays a significant role in the punctuated
equilibrium model of agenda-setting (Baumgartner et al., 2009; Jones
and Baumgartner, 2012). In this perspective information concerning
the exogenous shock (see focusing events below) is imported into the
policymaking system and depending on how the information is understood and processed it will produce some action, and perhaps very
high levels of action, from policymakers. Even then the system will
tend to revert toward something approaching the status quo ante without reinforcement.

The conservatism of most decision-making in punctuated equilibrium models can be seen as having much the same root as incremental

theories of policy (Dahl and Lindblom, 1953; Lindblom, 1965). Given the huge number of decisions with which policymakers must contend on a regular basis, and the complexity of each of those individual decisions, policymakers adopt simplifying rules of thumb that enable them to contend with policy. This means that most decisions being made are made incrementally, with small movements from the status quo, a style that preserves much of the existing policy frame. This tendency is heightened by the domination of policy areas by specific interests and the negative feedback that may result from attempts at change (McCool, 1998).

Given the tendency of negative feedback and incremental decisions to maintain particular patterns of policy, once attention is focused on the existing policy then the change that is triggered is likely to be extensive. That trigger may be from a focusing event (see below) or perhaps from greater general awareness of problems in the policy area. Once the interests and leaders who have been protecting the policy subsystem from external influences are incapable of maintaining that isolation, then the problems that may be pent up within the area become more widely apparent.

Somewhat analogously to Down's idea of "alarmed discovery", once the underlying policy problems do become salient they tend to result in what scholars working in this approach have called "disproportionate information processing" (Workman et al., 2009). That is, whether because of the accretion of problems or simply the opportunity to address issues that had been protected from broader consideration by members of the subsystem, there tends to be a large-scale response to the available information in the field, and perhaps non-incremental change. Again, however, that spate of change will tend to be short-lived, with a return to quiescence when other issues take center stage in the policy world.

The mass media and other sources of information are major players in the issue attention cycle. In some instances the media can be the source of the attention focused on the policy area. In other cases the media may merely reflect changes in attitudes and concerns among the public. At times the shift in attention may be the product of political entrepreneurs who press for opening the policy subsystem or the pressure may come from social movements. However the change is initiated, the shift away from incremental decision-making to more significant change represents an opening of agendas for change, albeit one likely to be followed by another period of incremental changes.

Focusing events and agenda-setting

The use of so-called focusing events is a special case of the agenda-setting process. As already noted above, proclaiming a problem or an issue a crisis can be a useful technique for placing an item on to the agenda, but there are also genuine crises and other extraordinary events that require governments to move out of their well-established routines and add new items to the agenda for action. The analysis of these events began with their definition in John Kingdon's seminal work on agendas (Kingdon, 1985 [2003]), and were seen as providing a "little push" from events that can permit individuals who have ideas about policy the opportunity to move those items from some limbo populated by good ideas into active consideration.

While Kingdon proposed this concept, it remained rather vague (see Birkland and de Young, 2013). To some extent it conflates sudden, major events with more gradual learning about policy opportunities and options (May, 1992). It also tends to conflate natural events and crises with opportunities for policy action created by intentional mobilization of interests, for example, the civil rights or anti-war movements. Finally, the idea has relatively little predictive capacity, although one can argue that such an event did occur after the fact. Why do some events produce major policy shifts and others do not? This concept, and Kingdon's analysis of it, do not provide a ready answer to that question.

Birkland (1998) discusses "potential focusing events" and considers why some events are effective in moving an issue on to an active agenda and others are not. The answer to this question is complex but somewhat like the punctuated equilibrium model discussed above. The cumulation of problems and their revelation, along with potential solutions tend to produce policy change (Birkland, 2006). Again, negative outcomes and failure tend to drive issues back on to the policy agenda to a greater extent than the opportunities to improve policies that are working reasonably well (Best, 2010). The familiar adage of "If it ain't broke don't fix it" appears to work in policy as well as other areas of human endeavor.

It is also important to note that focusing on policy problems may not just be a function of cataclysmic events. Sometimes it may be a simple act of civil disobedience such as Rosa Parks on the city bus in Montgomery, Alabama. Or it may be the publication of a book like Rachel Carson's Silent Spring or the decision of a vegetable seller in Tunisia that he could no longer accept repression by the government. It is almost impossible to predict when an event or any other action will produce a disproportionate policy response. What does seem clear, however, is that there are powerful forces maintaining the status quo that may require some spark – natural or human – to overcome.

Further, institutional structures may facilitate or reduce the impact of focusing events on policy change. The more organizations and institutions that are involved in the process of recognizing and then acting upon focusing events, the less likely there is to be quick, and perhaps disproportionate, response to the event (Maor, 2013). Similarly, focusing events that fall between the conventional "silos" of government may be less likely to provoke a strong response from the policymaking system.

Framing

Much of the above discussion of agenda-setting has taken as a given the nature of the issues being considered. While for many well-established policy problems that may not be a particular concern, for newer issues coming on to the agenda their definition cannot be assumed. And even for more established issues changing politics, and changes in the economy and society, may alter the manner in which the issues are regarded. Thus, in order to understand the process through which issues are placed on to an agenda, and the form in which these issues actually appear on those agendas, understanding how they are "framed" is important.

At the extreme, issues must be framed to appear on the policy agenda, or even to be recognized as a problem. For example, while spousal abuse is now widely recognized as a policy problem, in earlier times this behavior was largely assumed to be a normal part of family life (Baker, 2006). Therefore, for governments to be able to criminalize the actions, and to provide more supportive forms of intervention for the victims, this behavior had to be framed as a problem, and then as a public problem. The same pattern has been identified for child abuse (Nelson, 1984) and for abuse of the elderly, with these problems remaining widely accepted until political agitation identified them as major social problems.

Framing is important in the initial movement of an issue on to an active agenda of institutions in government, but it is also significant as a mechanism for understanding policy change and creating coordination among programs. One possible cause of an absence of coordination and cooperation among programs and organizations is that they represent different ideas and different frames of reference (see Bardach, 1998). For example, although social policies and labor market policies may have some common goals, and some common clients, they tend to have very different underlying ideas about the causes of unemployment, inequality and poverty.

Even when policy issues have been accepted on to the agenda, and have been framed as an issue suitable for public sector intervention, the question of framing has not been answered entirely. It is not only a question that there is an issue, the real problem arises when there are multiple interpretations of the issue. The classic example of this framing problem is drug policy (see Payan, 2006). This issue is usually addressed as a problem of law enforcement. There are, however, several other possible frames for this issue. For example, drugs constitute a major health issue, and also may be a consequence of social problems such as family breakdown and abuse.

These several possible frames for drug issues, and indeed multiple frames for any policy problem, can engender political conflicts. Many of these conflicts are organizational, given that the frame selected as the definition of, and remedy for, the perceived problem will determine which organizations within government will receive the funds and the personnel allocations associated with the program. While that conflict may be driven by utilitarian goals, there are also genuine policy debates over the best way to address the problem. Policy organizations are not only committed to their self-preservation and growth, they are also committed to ideas and to means of addressing policy problems.

The differences in possible frames for policy pose problems for policymaking. Donald Schön and Martin Rein (1994) have argued that reframing is a viable means of addressing difficult policy problems, especially those such as drug policy involving fundamental conflict of values and conceptions of what the policy problem may be. While in principle developing a frame for policy that could be acceptable to all participants has the potential of producing an enduring solution to policy conflicts, it also can be difficult to produce. If the organizations and individuals working in the policy area had such basic disagreements about the policy then finding a frame that is agreeable to all is a major challenge.

Summary

Agenda-setting is a crucial activity for policymaking. Unless an issue actually makes it to an active agenda it is not capable of being addressed through the policy process. Placing the issues on an agenda may appear rather simple, but actually may involve substantial political mobilization. There are numerous barriers to having any issue placed on the agenda, and those barriers may be even higher if the issue conflicts with the interests and values of economic and political elites.

But simply getting the issue on to an active agenda is only one aspect of the political process. Another question revolves around the nature of the issue when it actually arrives on that agenda. The process of framing the issue shapes the politics of the issue, both at the mass level and the organizational level. Political interests that want to prevail at the final adoption of the policy therefore must invest time and resources in the process of framing. Further, to produce policy change for existing programs reframing may be required, involving some of the same aspects of the initial process.

In terms of the design approach being used in this book, framing and agenda-setting more generally are the ways in which policy problems are interpreted so that they can be acted upon in the remaining parts of the policy process. Whereas the previous chapter has attempted to define these problems in more or less analytic and objective ways, what may ultimately matter is the way in which the issues are understood as they are processed through the political system. Understanding the technical nature of the issues can be important for policy analysts but in the end politics may be trumps and the political framing of an issue may matter most for the final policy emerging from the process.

NOTES

1 Despite that, critics such as E.E. Schattschneider (1962, p. 58) argue that "the flaw in pluralist heaven is that the heavenly chorus sings with a strong upper-class accent".

2 For example, corporatism and corporate pluralism in Northern Europe allow for a large range of actors to be involved in policymaking. In this case, in contrast to the usual critique of pluralism, this second pillar of democracy has tended to empower business and agricultural interests against the dominant role of labor and the political left in the electoral institutions.

PART II

Policy interventions

5 Designing intervention and implementation

Once policies are formulated, legitimated and have resources attached to them the task of actually delivering public services has to some extent only begun. The basic design of intervention may be contained in part within the formulation, but the implementation process itself requires careful design and consideration. Although implementation is sometimes dismissed as "mere administration" in reality administration is far from "mere" and the final impact of policies may be shaped as much by the manner of implementation as by the formal design of the programs. If we return to that initial definition of policy and politics as "Who Gets What" then the final decisions about those allocations may be made through implementation.

In addition to the direct impact that implementation has on the distribution of benefits and costs among members of the public, implementation of this process also affects the overall legitimacy and policy capacity of political systems. The majority of contacts between the state and the society come through the public bureaucracy during the process of implementation. These contacts provide the public with a sense of the probity, representativeness (see Peters et al., 2013) and responsiveness of the bureaucracy. A number of studies of the public bureaucracy have indicated that their treatment of citizens is reflected in their evaluations of the public sector, and therefore in the legitimacy of that political system.

In design terms, implementation should be considered as a central component of a more general intervention strategy. It is relatively simple to say that policymakers want to alter the behavior of individuals in some manner, or they want to shape the economy in certain ways. It is more difficult to determine how those changes can be actually brought to fruition. At what points in the underlying social and economic processes is it most effective and efficient to intervene? And through what mechanisms? And what are the barriers to making those interventions effective? This chapter and the next will discuss interventions designed to produce change. This chapter will discuss implementation in general, and the following chapter will discuss policy instruments as an important analytic approach to the process of implementation.

Much of the discussion of implementation could be characterized as "the horrors of war" (Linder and Peters, 1987). The study of the concept was initiated by examining failure (Pressman and Wildavsky, 1974), and much of the subsequent literature has also focused on failures to implement successfully. This emphasis on failure appears in other areas of policy studies (Bovens and 't Hart, 1996) but has been a dominant theme in the study of implementation. That emphasis on failure may reflect in part the difficulties inherent in implementation, as well as an intellectual perspective that demands perfect implementation. That intellectual perspective was informed in part by a legalistic perspective that assumes perfect compliance with law, even if that law is vague and perhaps unenforceable (Lane, 1983).

Although interventions and implementation remain a central component of the policy process the academic interest in implementation has to some extent waned. This declining interest may merely represent fad and fashion in policy studies, but also represent some of the research difficulties involved in identifying the effects of administration on policy outcomes. To be able to understand why programs are not as effective as hoped by their "formators" requires tracking through the process of implementation, much like the original Pressman and Wildavsky study. Even then, any failures in the policy may not be attributable entirely to implementation failures. The need to rely heavily on case studies and the difficulties in assigning causation make implementation incompatible with the canons of much of contemporary social science.

The above being said, there has been some revival of interest in implementation (Winter, 2011) that has addressed some of the fundamental administrative and policy issues involved in this stage of the policy process. For example, there has been greater investment in understanding compliance with law and the associated effects on implementation (Saetren, 2014). In addition, there has been a revival of theorizing about street-level bureaucracy (Hupe and Buffat, 2014) and with that more general consideration of the discretion, and the control of discretion, among the lower echelons of civil servants (Maynard-Mooney and Musheno, 2003; Brodkin, 2011).[1]

Implementation as a component of the policy process

Governments have been implementing policies for as long as they have been in the business of governing. Few if any programs can make themselves perform automatically, so some means of having them achieve their objectives must be devised. The principal actor in implementing programs in government is the public bureaucracy. That said, however, increasingly the public sector utilizes non-governmental actors to assist in implementation, or even to be the primary source of implementation. And even if the public sector does retain control over implementation it is unlikely that any single organization is fully responsible for administration of public programs, and therefore implementation involves the interaction of a number of organizations and even individual actors.

Implementation outcomes as probabilities

The multiplicity of actors involved in implementation motivated the initial discussion of this concept by Pressman and Wildavsky (1974). Prior to their popularizing the term "implementation" the activity of translating programs into action would have been discussed as just plain public administration. Pressman and Wildavsky, however, emphasized the difficulties involved in making programs work, especially in the multi-organizational environment that characterizes most public programs. The extensive subtitle to their book emphasized that good policy ideas often do not go into effect as planned, and that scholars and practitioners need to understand those implementation failures.

To understand the difficulties involved in implementation Pressman and Wildavsky developed the concept of "clearance points".[2] These were points along the process of implementation at which a positive decision was required for the process to continue as expected by the "formators" of the process. This analysis indicates just how complex implementation can be, especially in a federal country such as the United States (see also Hanf and Toonen, 1985; Doonan, 2013). In their study of the implementation of an economic development program developed in the federal government in the San Francisco Bay area, Pressman and Wildavsky identified over one hundred clearance points at which the implementation process could have been stalled and killed, whether intentionally or simply by lethargy or poor administration.

The problem presented to policymakers by the large number of clearance points in programs such as the program discussed by Pressman and Wildavsky is that one of these may be sufficient to derail a program. Even if actors at each of these clearance points are in fact committed to making the program work and are skilled administrators there is still some possibility that implementation will not be successful. Even if the probability of successful implementation at each clearance point is 0.99 then the probability of successfully implementing through 100 points is less than 0.00001. Implementation therefore requires active political involvement if the program adopted by some organization in government is actually to go into effect in the field.

The need for political involvement in pushing through the implementation process raises the question of just how to alter the behavior of actors involved in making these decisions. Elinor Bowen (1982) began with the fundamental conception about implementation used by Pressman and Wildavsky and then developed ideas about how the active implementer could overcome some of the difficulties identified in the original research on implementation. Rather than accepting passively that there is a chance of failure at each stage the would-be implementer can affect the process positively and increase the possibilities for success.

For example, that active implementer could attempt to create a bandwagon effect, using success at some clearance points to create momentum that could be used to spur other actors to accept the program. That implementer can also be persistent, and not take no as the final answer when implementation fails at one point. That implementer can also attempt to skip over potential bottlenecks in the process to place pressure on the recalcitrant actors. There are other tactics that can be used but the basic point is that any simple, passive conception of implementation does not take into account the possibilities for moving the process forward even in the face of apparent opposition.[3] This argument also emphasizes the extent to which implementation, and other aspects of public administration, are fundamentally political activities.

Forward and backward mapping for design

The initial discussion of implementation was conducted as if this component of the political process were simply an exercise in probability theory. This perspective involved relatively little sense of design but instead tended to take both the political structure and the process of implementation largely as givens. While that analysis provides a background against which to compare the realities of administering policies, it does little to help policymakers who may be attempting to develop a strategy for intervention and implementation.

A second stage in the development of thinking about implementation represented more of an attempt to assist would-be implementers in building more effective systems for putting their programs into effect. Most thinking about making public policies assumes that the formulators of the policy decide what they want to do, and then attempt to put those policies into effect. That image of policymaking to some extent conforms to a democratic vision of governance in which elected officials make policies and then work to implement those policies.[4]

One proposal for designing programs for enhanced implementation was discussed as "backward mapping" (Elmore, 1985). To some extent this proposal involves taking the idea of clearance points from Pressman and Wildavsky and thinking about what can be done in the design of programs to minimize the negative impact of those constraints on implementation. The basic idea is to consider what the actors implementing a prospective program prefer and designing the program around those preferences. The fundamental goals of the program would be driven by perceived needs to intervene, but structure of that intervention might be shaped more by the preferences of the implementers, and the preferences of the target population.

From a design perspective on public policy backward mapping makes a great deal of sense. Rather than thinking about the formulation of a program in an administrative vacuum backward mapping considers the likelihood of success of an intervention. This strategy for shaping programs at least in part on the basis of the probabilities of implementation success may increase the overall success of the programs. In addition, this perspective on implementation corresponds well with the more evolutionary discussion of policy, assuming that firm designs are difficult to achieve within the complexities of the political world, and the even more complex social and economic systems. Therefore, this potential linking of formulation with the targets through considering feasibility may open the way for more adaptive policy.

Although seemingly desirable from the design perspective, backward mapping also tends to imply that policies would be driven by feasibility rather than by policy priorities. It is not difficult to argue that implementation is difficult and therefore finding means of reducing friction with both clients and implementers can be desirable. But as feasibility tends to dominate real policy preferences then the likelihood of producing effective programs and producing real changes in the target population is reduced.

Multiple actors: implementation structures and networks

As already discussed, almost any implementation effort will involve a number of actors. This observation is to some extent a defining feature of implementation studies, but it is also the foundation for several additional theoretical approaches to implementation. For the two approaches to implementation discussed here the fundamental question is understanding how the interactions among actors involved in implementation occur and how they shape the outcomes of the administrative process.

The more basic of these approaches is concerned with "implementation structures" as the defining feature of the process of putting programs into effect. Bennie Hjern and David Porter (1981) argued very early in the study of implementation that "the single lonely organization" is dead and that it had been replaced by structures involving a number of actors. The death of that single organization may be exaggerated, and there are certainly cases in which implementation is confined to one organization,[5] but implementation tends to involve increasing numbers of actors.

While the large number of actors involved in many attempts at implementation may create problems, as indicated by Pressman and Wildavsky and all implementation scholars since, it is also possible to exaggerate those difficulties. Bowen pointed to several means that implementers could employ to avoid passive acceptance of the impacts of clearance points, and other students of implementation have also pointed to means of pushing the process forward even against opposition (Hill and Hupe, 2014).

The potential problems created by multiple actors in implementation are also mitigated in part because these actors are not drawn at random at the outset of each new program, but rather represent institutionalized patterns of interaction (Peters, 2014b). The organizations and other actors involved in implementing social programs, or any other type of program, in a community tend to work together for an extended period of time and often work together on a number of different programs. They therefore develop routinized patterns of interaction and generally develop trust among themselves. Both routines and trust reduce transaction costs among the participants (Calista, 1994) and make implementation proceed more smoothly. This institutionalization does not mean that stability and comity will be preserved across all programs, but it does serve as a good starting point for implementing programs.

Conceptualizing multi-actor implementation as networks is yet another variation in this general theme (O'Toole, 2011). Network theory has become increasingly important in the study of public policy and governance (see Sørenson and Torfing, 2007), and this approach has been applied to implementation in a number of settings. Further, network thinking about implementation tends to integrate some aspects of the backward mapping approach as network actors tend to be involved in the formulation of policies as well as in their implementation. Therefore, the members of the networks to some extent are designing policies in ways that will help themselves as actors involved in the implementation of those programs.

Network implementation implies a number of actors working together to implement a program. The assumption in these models is that networks are composed of relatively equal actors who bargain among themselves to deliver the program in question. In the other models, even that of implementation structures, there is an assumption that the process is driven by government actors. In the extreme, non-governmental actors are conceptualized as much as potential barriers to the process as they are partners in producing the program. In less extreme views, the social and market actors are partners involved in implementing programs designed primarily within the public sector.

Summary

Beginning with the Pressman and Wildavsky study and moving through the other approaches to implementation, some common strands of analysis appear. Perhaps the most important of these is that implementation is a "game" with a large number of players (see Bardach, 1977), and understanding the interactions among the participants is crucial for understanding the outcomes. Further, this is a political process as well as an administrative process. The politics involved may be organizational rather than partisan, but they are still politics. And finally, because of the first two characteristics, simple legalistic conceptions of implementation are inadequate for understanding what actually happens.

Gaining compliance

Much of the discussion of implementation is done in terms of laws and the use of political and legal instruments to achieve policy goals. There is, however, also an important psychological element involved in implementation – the need for compliance by citizens and organizations. While the targets for policies may be threatened, coerced or cajoled into compliance with a law, it is much easier for governments attempting to implement the law if they can gain willing acceptance and compliance.

As much as being a characteristic of the policies in question, gaining compliance may be a function of the legitimacy of the programs and of government more generally. Some policy instruments – those relying on information and persuasion – are heavily dependent on the legitimacy of government, or perhaps on the legitimacy of the private sector organizations actually delivering the programs (see Chapter 6). For those instruments to gain compliance the organizations attempting the persuasion must be legitimate and accepted by the targets of the policy.

It is also important for program designers to realize that compliance through use of rigid enforcement and hierarchy may produce the desired outcome, but it can also be extremely expensive. That expense is not only in terms of the actual expenditure of resources in the public sector but also the potential loss of trust by citizens. Citizens may resent being forced into accepting programs and using more coercive instruments may make implementing other programs in the future even more difficult to implement.

Drift and sabotage

Even if the process of implementation does go forward, it is likely that the policy being implemented will to some extent be altered in the process. As already noted, the real policy is the policy that is implemented, and the complexity of the structures involved in the process tend to produce deviations from the intentions of the framers. At each of those clearance points decisions are being made and even if the actors involved are acting in good faith they may not interpret the intentions of the lawmakers correctly, or they are often faced with political pressures that reduce their cooperation.

The problem of multiple actors in the system for implementation can be seen through the lens of delegation and discretion. When laws are made and then are implemented through administrative organizations or non-governmental actors those implementing organizations are given discretion to make decisions. At the extreme, administrative organizations make many more rules than legislatures (Kerwin, 2011). And the implementation of programs is delegated to lower levels of public organizations as well as to quasi-autonomous agencies within government (Pollitt and Talbot, 2004).

Delegation to these organizations can leverage resources but may also produce difficulties in implementing programs in the manner desired by the legislature or other sources of legislation. The implementing organizations – whether within the public sector or in the private sector – will have their own values and their own priorities, and therefore will interpret legislation in ways that may not have been intended. One clear example of this has been the Environmental Protection Agency (EPA) in the United States interpreting its mandate on clean air to include carbon dioxide, hence providing a backdoor method for the Obama administration to address the issue of climate change (Wald, 2012).

The issue of bureaucratic "drift" in implementation, especially the implementation of regulatory policy, has been addressed by scholars advocating the development of "tamper-proof legal instruments" that can ensure that the program is implemented in the way intended (see McCubbins et al., 1989). These attempts to limit discretion represent the continuing conflict within government over implementing programs as intended by lawmakers and building in sufficient flexibility and discretion so that programs can adapt to changing circumstances. This is, of course, in part a political as well as an administrative battle – conservatives hated the use of discretion by the EPA mentioned above while liberals applauded it.

Barriers to implementation

The complexity and the attenuation of the implementation process are themselves fundamental barriers to effective implementation, but there are other factors in the process that can reduce even more the probability that legislation will be implemented as intended. These factors may to some extent be overcome through careful planning of the implementation strategy, but some may simply constitute problems that must be understood. Implementation is rarely perfect (see Hood, 1976) and those failures of implementation are often a major cause for failures in the policy process considered more broadly (McConnell, 2010).

Legislation

The legislation itself often constitutes a major barrier to effective implementation. Legislation almost inevitably represents compromises of political forces, and those compromises often produce vague legislation that cannot be implemented readily. Perhaps more accurately, the legislation may be so vague that it is difficult to determine if indeed it has been implemented effectively or not. Legislation often contains lofty goals necessary to have it passed, and which are useful for appealing to the voting public, but that rhetoric may be of little use to a civil servant attempting to put the program into effect.

In addition to the rhetorical flourishes that may be contained in legislation, legislation may also create extremely complex implementation structures. Perhaps the most egregious example of this complexity is the Affordable Care Act ("Obamacare") in the United States. This Act was over 1000 pages long and involved a variety of measures designed to alter the manner in which health care is financed and delivered. Even the centerpiece of the Act, the insurance exchanges, involved complex interactions between private insurers, potential purchasers and state (and the federal) governments. It is perhaps not surprising that the first few months of the program were, to say the least, trying (Clemmitt, 2014).

Finally, contrary to the logic of backward mapping, legislation may be written in ways that do not recognize the strengths and preferences of the organizations that will implement it. I have been making the point throughout this volume that organizations within government are crucial for the success of policies, and failure to take the preferences of those organizations into account can readily produce implementation failures. These difficulties in implementation may be manifested when there are sharp ideological differences between members of the implementing organization and the formulator,[6] but may occur simply when the designers of programs do not recognize the organizational routines and preferences for particular instruments that exist within most public organizations.

Politics

In addition to the coalition politics involved in the creation of legislation, other aspects of politics also make implementation difficult and sometimes move the program as implemented away from the intentions of the formulators of the program. These politically inspired deviations are most likely to appear in presidential and federal systems. In parliamentary systems the legislature and the executive responsible for implementation will almost certainly be aligned politically, whereas in presidential systems those institutions may have conflicting ideas about policies and their implementation. Further, most parliamentary systems are consensus systems (Lijphart, 1984) so that the policy change across governments tends to be less than in presidential systems that function more as majoritarian systems.

Inter-governmental relations may present a particular challenge for effective implementation in federal regimes (Stoker, 1991). The constitutional autonomy of sub-national units in federal systems, and the concurrent jurisdiction of levels of government over more policy areas, means that the central government is generally negotiating rather than mandating policies when working with sub-national governments.[7] However, implementation within systems of "multi-level governance" can be a challenge in any regime (Hooghe and Marks, 2003). Even if lower levels of government are controlled by the same political party they may still have different priorities from the central government and therefore may implement programs differently than intended. And if there are different political parties involved across the levels of government the threats to implementation are exacerbated.

Multiple actors

As governments begin to utilize more and more third-party actors to assist in implementation, or to take full responsibility for the implementation of public programs, potential barriers to effective implementation arise. Just as sub-national governments may have their own priorities and therefore attempt to implement public programs in their own ways, so too do third-party implementers – market or non-market – also have individual preferences and priorities, although there has been a great deal of enthusiasm concerning the involvement of networks and other social actors in implementation (O'Toole, 2000).

Although much of the discussion of multiple actors is based on potential problems with organizations in the private sector, reforms in the public sector have tended to create more problems of this sort within the public sector itself. Part of the logic of the New Public Management, beginning in the 1980s, is that efficiency and accountability in the public sector can be enhanced by dividing large public organizations into multiple single-purpose organizations usually called agencies (Laegreid and Verhoest, 2010). While these organizations may at times increase the efficiency of administration, their autonomy may also provide them more opportunities to make their own decisions about the interpretation of legislation. Indeed, their pursuit of efficiency in their own terms may undermine their willingness to pursue the collective goals of government.

Although we can think of the difficulties created by this multiplicity of organizations involved in implementation as purely an administrative issue, it can also have significant policy consequences. First, although usually discussed as leveraging private actors to improve policy, the involvement of multiple actors may create conflicts that in the end may lessen the success of a program. Further, implementation involves making policy as well as strictly putting a policy into effect, so that the intentions of the legislation may be altered when being implemented by individuals and groups with perhaps different policy values. While some of this same policy drift may occur when implementation is entirely within the public sector the drift may be less controllable when being produced by private actors.

Performance standards

Somewhat paradoxically the increased use of performance management as a part of the reforms associated with the New Public Management may actually reduce the capacity to implement programs as intended by the formulators of the policies. The basic logic of performance management is that by establishing standards and targets for the organizations and individuals responsible for implementation that implementation will be improved (Bouckaert and Halligan, 2007). While that goal is well intentioned, it may set up situations in which the quality of programs provided actually diminish.

The difficulty in performance management is that when people have to reach targets they will find ways to reach them, regardless of the actual effects on the intentions of the program (Radin, 2006). For example, if the police have a performance standard for clearing a certain percentage of reported crimes they may simply refuse to record some crimes that may be difficult to solve (Barrett, 2014). Or they may reclassify crimes as less serious so they can demonstrate that rates of serious crimes such as homicide are falling (Eterno and Silverman, 2012). And it is certainly not only the police who find ways to reach targets for implementation without actually implementing the programs as intended.

Street-level bureaucrats and implementation

Above we discussed some of the potential problems of drift in the implementation of public policies in general terms. Although there are a number of potential influences on implementation, the impact of the lower levels of the bureaucracy represents an especially important influence on the decisions that are finally made by governments. This influence highlights the point made above that the real policy of government (and its collaborators in the private sector) is the policy as it is implemented.

Despite attempts by legislatures and others who make law, discretion is always necessary in implementation. Indeed, legislatures may not want to write laws that are too precise and too detailed. They both lack the expertise in many (if not most) areas of policy but also are faced with social and technological circumstances that often change rapidly. Drug law enforcement makes this point rather clearly. Most countries outlaw the use of certain drugs, and place them on schedules of differing degrees of severity for punishment. This worked reasonably well until drug dealers found ways to alter a chemical compound slightly, making it outside the law but having the same effects as the illegal substance (McElroy, 2013). Lacking discretion to confiscate any drug that appears harmful, enforcers must wait for new law.

The impact of the lower echelons of bureaucracy – the "street-level bureaucrats" – on policy is apparent in social policy and in regulatory policy. The term was coined by Michael Lipsky (1980) primarily in relation to social policy. He was concerned with the extent to which workers in social service organizations could bend the rules either positively or negatively and therefore advantage or disadvantage clients.[8] His research, and a good deal of other research on the powers even of receptionists in social service organizations, indicates the extent to which clients may be vulnerable, and programs vulnerable to sabotage.

The lower echelon of workers in regulatory organizations also have substantial discretion in making decisions, and therefore a good deal of power. Research in a number of settings (Lundqvist, 1980; Bardach and Kagan, 1982, 2009) has pointed out that inspectors have a good deal of discretion in how they administer environmental and health and safety laws. Further, exercising that discretion is often key to the success of programs, as excessive rigidity in the rules may lead to inspectors ignoring violations that could have disastrous consequences for a regulated industry. The capacity to negotiate enforcement can lead to more effective policy implementation,[9] although it may also result in deviations from the intentions of the formulators of the policy.

Just as the New Public Management mentioned above has tended to enhance the autonomy of agencies delivering public services, the "empowerment" strand of reform in the public sector (see Peters, 2001a; Fernandez and Moldogazie, 2011) has tended to give lower-level officials within organizations of all sorts greater autonomy to make their own decisions. Thus, a great deal of the change within the public sector over the past several decades has tended to delegate more and therefore to make implementation more difficult for legislatures and political executives to control. This in turn means that policy outcomes for citizens are likely to be more variable, raising significant questions of accountability and even of democracy.

What is implementation success?

All the above discussions of implementation have discussed the process of implementation, and many, if not most, of these have described the outcomes of that process as failures. Indeed, most studies of implementation have emphasized failures and discussed how and why implementation fails. While those failures are often obvious, in many other cases they may be in the eye of the beholder. The question of implementation failure is important for understanding policy success and failure more generally.

Implementation failure is not just a simple empirical question, but rather the failure is related to the numerous theoretical approaches to implementation. If one adopts the top-down perspective then failure can be seen as a policy outcome that does not conform to the intentions of the initial policy formulation. If, however, one has a more flexible, bottom-up perspective then failure is more difficult to define, and also less likely to occur. These two fundamental theoretical approaches then are also potentially related to different approaches to measurement, in degree if not in type.

These alternative conceptions of success in implementation can be related to the fundamental issue of policy design. The more constrained top-down conception of implementation success is derived from the more rigid conception of policy design, assuming that initial design perspectives will be carried through the process. In such a view implementation failure implies a failure of the initial design. On the other hand, if one adopts a more argumentative perspective then the program may evolve more as it is implemented (but see Brown and Wildavsky, 1984). Rather than being set rigidly by decisions at the outset the policy inevitably adapts, with bottom-up implementation representing one dimension of that adaptation.

From either perspective, there is still not a clear measure of what would constitute failure. Even in the top-down perspective it is not clear how much drift constitutes failure. Any demand for perfect implementation of a policy would appear unreasonable, given the complexity of the process and the difficulties in affecting large-scale social and economic processes. On the other hand, simply saying that something happened, and perhaps something good happened, seems too weak a criterion to argue that implementation has been successful. Further, does one attribute success or failure to the implementation process or to the initial policy design? These difficulties then constitute a useful place at which to begin the final section of this book – the role of evaluation in the policy process.

Interventions and implementation

The title for this chapter includes the word "intervention", although almost all the discussion until this point concerns implementation. Thinking about how to intervene effectively into ongoing social and economic processes involves design elements such as policy instruments, but may also require thinking about broader implementation strategies as well. These intervention strategies to a great extent mirror the implementation literature, with three broad conceptions about how to put policies into action in their socio-economic environment, and indeed within the political system itself.

The first and dominant strategy remains one depending on law and formal hierarchy to achieve policy goals. The foundation of the implementation literature is an assumption (unstated at times) that laws should, and could, be implemented perfectly with the intentions of the framers of the legislation going into effect. Implementation in this context is assumed to be done primarily or totally by the public sector itself. The policy might still fail, but it would not fail because of implementation deficiencies. Especially in administrative and political systems that are highly legalistic, this conception of implementation persists, and the probability of perceived implementation failure is consequently greater (Hammerschmid and Meyer, 2004).

The second significant strategy for implementation emphasizes an understanding of the context into which a policy is being introduced. The fundamental idea of backward mapping is to understand the environment of policy and then design programs that will be most acceptable within that environment (Elmore, 1985). While this strategy may lead to greater implementation success, there is a clear question of whether it can produce policy success. That is, if the program is designed for easy implementation and for acceptability, it may not be capable of addressing the underlying problems it was meant to solve.

The backward-mapping approach to intervention also points to the potential danger of the term "feasibility" in policy analysis (Meltsner, 1972; Vanderbroght and Yamasaki, 2004). One almost sure way to defeat a policy proposal is to say that it is not feasible. That judgment of a lack of feasibility may be passed without any great analytic support, or it may be expressed in political rather than analytic terms, but in either case it is a rather facile means of defeating a program. While backward mapping may still lead to the adoption of a program, that program may be so watered-down that its success may be relatively insignificant.

The third approach to implementation is also concerned with context and the socio-economic environment of policy, but tends to use the social actors rather than to have policy necessarily shaped by them. The use of horizontal patterns of implementation involving networks and market actors may facilitate policy delivery, if not have policies shaped ex ante by those socio-economic forces. Of course during implementation the social and market actors will almost certainly influence the nature of the policy as it actually goes into effect "on the ground". We should in fact expect more drift from the intentions of the framers of the legislation, an outcome that can be compensated for by the ability to leverage the resources of the non-governmental actors involved.

These implementation strategies may also be seen as broad strategies for intervention, and for policy design more generally. One version of policymaking would be an étatiste form of governing almost entirely through public sector institutions, using law and hierarchy for control over the society. An alternative could be seen as permitting self-regulation of the society with very loose guidance based on guidelines, frameworks and so on. And finally policy may be pursued through collaboration with social and market actors, attempting to direct those actors in the direction of legislative and administrative goals, but also recognizing the importance of the interactions between state and society.

However governments and their allies attempt to govern and to make and implement policy, it is not an easy task. The implementation literature has emphasized those difficulties and the significant probability of failure. That sense of failure, however, may be a product of high expectations and a legalistic frame of reference that assumes that there should be little deviation in the implemented programs from the formal law. But we are still left with little guidance in understanding what is adequate implementation, and when failure has indeed occurred. And further, despite the numerous failures in perfect implementation, there are still important successes and many policies do work.

Summary

If public policies are to mean anything they must be implemented. That is, however, easier said than done, and the history of the study of implementation is built primarily on the study of failure. That emphasis on failure is, however, perhaps excessively negative. Governments have been able to make programs work, and sometimes work very well, although few if any programs are implemented in exactly the manner in which they were intended. Thus, while failure has helped to bring scholarly attention to the issue of implementation in reality the outcomes are much more mixed.

The study of implementation also emphasizes the complexity of public policy. Whether the actors involved are public, private or a combination, almost all implementation involves multiple actors interacting in a variety of ways for the program to function. Recognizing the existence of these multiple actors in the process emphasizes the importance of discretion in implementation, and the extent to which policies may change during implementation as a result of that delegation. That change does not mean failure, but does invoke the need to evaluate what has happened and to use that evaluation to continue improving policy.

NOTES

1 This concern about discretion was in part sparked by administrative reforms during the latter part of the twentieth century that encouraged delegation and empowerment for lower echelon workers in government.

2 This concept is similar to the concept of "veto points" in institutional theory developed by Tsebelis (2000).

3 Ernst Alexander (1989) argues that Bowen's optimism is founded on a set of assumptions about the malleability of the implementation process that may be applicable in only a limited number of circumstances. His argument, and hers, are indicative of marked contrasts in views about the formality of public administration.

4 It in some ways conforms even more to patterns of policymaking in less democratic regimes in which the hegemonic party, or the individual hegemon, will expect his or her policies to be implemented without question.

5 For example, most tax legislation is implemented by a single powerful organization rather than by multiple, dispersed organizations. That said, the private industry of accountants, lawyers and advisors that attempts to lessen the tax liabilities of individuals and corporations must be considered participants in the process.

6 For example, the EPA in the United States pushed back rather hard against the intentions of several Republican presidents to weaken environmental programs.

7 The level of control of the center does vary significantly within federal regimes (see Fenna and Hueglin, 2010).

8 For a very negative conception of this role of social service workers see Piven and Cloward (1993).

9 This acceptance of negotiation also becomes crucial for writing regulations, as "soft law" becomes more widely accepted. See Mörth (2004) and Dahl and Hansen (2006).

6 Policy instruments

The preceding chapter discussed implementation and intervention in a relatively general manner, but we now need to consider more carefully the means through which that implementation is conducted. Public programs are in essence designed using policy instruments, or tools, for implementation. These tools (see Hood, 1976; Salamon, 2001a; Hood and Margetts, 2007) are necessary to take the intentions of legislators or other "formators" of policy and translate them into effective action.

This point about the central role of policy instruments appears rather simple, but behind that apparent simplicity lies a good deal of complexity. Policy instruments are not simple, mechanical means of intervention, but have political impacts of their own. Further, they can be evaluated along a number of different dimensions and there may be little agreement on the desirability of one over another in specific policy situations. Finally, instruments themselves involve a number of different underlying mechanisms for affecting the society, and these need to be understood in order to make informed choices about instruments.

Perhaps even more basically, to be successful policy instruments require compliance from the members of the society. In some societies that is relatively easy, and governments are able to use relatively "soft" policy instruments because they can be sure the public will obey laws. In other societies, however, direct command and control, and direct enforcement, may be required to get the public to obey laws (Salamon, 2001b; Héritier and Rhodes, 2012). And of course the targets of the laws being imposed may affect these choices, with most people readily complying with laws against murder but relatively fewer citizens being willing to obey speed laws.

This chapter will discuss the role that policy instruments play in implementing policy, and how they relate to more general designs for policy interventions. This discussion will require first categorizing the instruments, then discussing how to select them for utilization in a policy design and then evaluating them. The selection of instruments is a function of a number of factors, which emphasize the political dimensions of instrument selection. That evaluation is multi-faceted, so that instruments that are evaluated well on one dimension may be rated poorly on others. Further, that evaluation of instruments is contingent, so an instrument that may be evaluated positively in some circumstances may be considered negatively in others.

I am discussing policy instruments in the context of implementation, but we could also address them as a major subject of policy formulation. Policy designers have to select not only the more general nature of the program but also the individual instruments that are used to achieve the goals of the program (James and Jorgensen, 2009). As described earlier when discussing agenda-setting, excluding options from consideration can be a significant means of controlling the outcomes of the selection process. In this case, however, the principal actors involved may be policy advisors and public administrators who present policy options, and instrument options, to the political leaders who in general are responsible for the choices. Thus, the exclusion of instruments may bias policy outcomes just as much as the exclusion of issues at the agenda-setting stage.

Classifying policy instruments

Governments have a very large tool chest at their disposal as they attempt to influence the society and economy. Each of these tools are not, however, sui generis but rather fall into a number of categories. These categories are useful not just for academic discussions of public policy but also for designing public policies. In addition, the categories of instruments help in understanding the underlying nature of the instruments and their linkages with other instruments. Further, it helps to understand both the effectiveness of instruments as well as the politics involved in their selection. Again, these instruments are not neutral tools like a hammer but have their own political economies.

In this discussion of policy instruments we will need to remember that the tools are to some extent empty vessels into which a good deal of additional policy content must be poured. For example, we can say that government is using a tax instrument to achieve some policy purpose. That is helpful, but is it an income tax or an expenditure tax? And if it is an expenditure tax is it a general imposition or an excise tax affecting only a limited number of products? And is that excise tax levied at the point of sale or earlier in the distribution process (like the value-added tax) so that the consumer is not necessarily aware of the scale of the tax being charged? The fine print of an instrument is important, so as we discuss a range of instruments (Table 6.1) it is important to remain cognizant of the internal variations.

The first significant attempt at classification, or at least enumeration, of the policy instruments available to government was supplied by E.S. Kirschen (1964) and his colleagues. This effort listed 64 alternative policy instruments, all considered options for economic policy. Thus, even within one policy domain, albeit an important one, there is a very large number of options for the public sector to intervene. This enumeration is perhaps too extensive, but it does demonstrate the wide array of options for governments, and these were indeed for governments and did not include many alternative forms of intervention.

While the simple enumeration of policy instruments may not appear to advance the cause of policy analysis, it is still important to understand just what options are available to decision-makers who want to design a policy program. Table 6.1 provides a list of instruments arranged within some broad categories. This listing contains the principal policy instruments but each of these might be further differentiated. In short, there is no shortage of ways for governments to intervene, so we must now consider how policy designers should choose their instruments when they formulate policy.

Political science approaches to instruments

For political scientists and public administration scholars Christopher Hood's book The Tools of Government (1976) represented the first

Table 6.1   Examples of types of policy instruments

Economic	Legal	Persuasive	Other
Grants	Regulation	Information	Monitoring
Subsidies	Contracts	"Nudges"	
Taxes			
Tax expenditures			

significant discussion of instruments and their role in policy implementation. Rather than begin with a simple enumeration of policy instruments, Hood began by considering the more basic resources available to governments. He classified these using the acronym NATO, meaning Nodality (Information), Authority, Treasure and Organization. In other words, governments can use information, legal authority, money and people to influence their surrounding society.

As well as these four categories of the resources available to governments, Hood argued that instruments could be considered as "detectors" or "effectors". We tend to think of policy instruments primarily as producing change in the environment (effectors), but they can also be used to detect changes in that environment. For example, government personnel are in touch with their clients or are patrolling neighborhoods (police) and hence know what is happening within the society that may require intervention. This role of detection is perhaps as important for instruments as producing change, because if government is blind to environmental change it is unlikely to make good policy decisions.

The Hood taxonomy of policy instruments, or perhaps more precisely the resources of government, also makes it obvious that the majority of the programs actually used by government are hybrids, involving more than one of those basic resources. For example, tax expenditures are obviously dependent on Treasure, but also require monitoring (Nodality). They, and any tax, depend on the legal authority of government, and finally tax authorities (Organizations) monitor and perhaps directly implement those laws. Thus, although the resources of government can be separated analytically, and that separation is useful for the analyst, in practice individual tools involve some or all of those resources.

Hood's four categories of tools, or resources, was the beginning for other categorizations of policy instruments in political science. One classification (Bemelmans-Videc et al., 1998) described instruments as "Carrots, Sticks, and Sermons". An even simpler categorization (Gormley, 1989) was that instruments can be understood as "Muscles and Prayers". The latter dichotomy makes the point that government can either choose to exercise its power or it can merely rely on moral suasion to attempt to gain compliance. The former classification differentiates the use of government power into incentives and disincentives, but at times the only option is to preach at the public.

The above classifications of instruments emphasize the mechanisms of intervention, but instruments can also be classified according to their political and social characteristics. In particular, some scholars have argued that the most appropriate way to understand instruments is through the level of legitimate coercion they impose on actors in the society. Their argument (Macdonald, 2001) is that less coercive instruments are, all else being equal, more acceptable in liberal societies than the more coercive. In this context instruments can be classified from self-regulation at one end of the continuum and direct government provision of a service at the other.

Yet another classification system (McDonnell and Elmore, 1987) contains four major categories – mandates, inducements, capacity-building and system-changing. These two scholars were working primarily in education policy, but their scheme has relevance beyond that one area. Perhaps the most significant element in this analysis is the difference made between individuals as the targets of the instruments and institutions or systems as the focus of change. This analysis makes the point that although we tend to think about changing individual behavior or the outcomes for individuals with policy, the most efficient way of doing so may be to address deficiencies at the systemic level. This emphasis on process and the environment of decisions is echoed in part in Michael Howlett's (2001) concept of procedural policy instruments. His argument is that each of the four categories in the NATO scheme has procedural as well as substantive elements, and indeed each of those can be further divided into positive and negative.

Finally, Lester Salamon (2001b) has labeled tools as simply "old" and "new". This is not as simple a classification as it appears, given that what is meant by old in this case are instruments that depend heavily on command and control. The new policy instruments, on the other hand, depend more on negotiation and collaboration. These new instruments are, in other terms, "soft law" rather than hard law (Mörth, 2004). As with the classification based on coerciveness described above, the assumption is that the degree of intrusiveness and control is central to understanding policy instruments, and further contemporary politics and society are more resistant to the direct use of government power than was true in the past.[1]

Constructivist perspectives on instruments

In addition to the classification schemes based on more or less objective characteristics of policy instruments, other scholars have argued that instruments are best understood in constructivist terms (see Bressers and Klok, 1988). That is, most categorizations of instruments assume that the instruments have objective characteristics that will produce relatively similar consequences regardless of the setting within which they are being utilized. The constructivist position, analogous to some of the framing literature mentioned above, is that policy instruments are generally discussed in objective terms, but they can also be seen as social and political constructs.

For example, Lascoumbes and Le Gales (2007) point to the extent to which most studies of instruments have tended to look at them in a rather technical manner. They argue that instruments, like other aspects of policy, need to be understood in a political and social context as well as simple "tools". The tools metaphor has been useful, but may undervalue the political aspects of these means of creating public action. Further, the focus on individual tools tends to undervalue the importance of constructing policy mixes that involve multiple instruments. Even a simple tools logic might alert the designer that not all instruments will work together easily, but the more political and constructivist position may make the need to consider interactions even more visible.

The psychology and sociology of instruments: nudge and its allies

There has been increasing interest in a set of tools relying on psychological rather than more material forces to produce the desired outcomes on behalf of the public sector (Thalen and Sunstein, 2008). The basic idea of nudge is to provide subtle incentives and disincentives to the public to get them to behave in the ways desired by policymakers without having major intrusions, or at least obvious intrusions. In this way nudge is perhaps at an even further end of the intrusiveness scale than the examples given by Salamon. For example, rather than having real police personnel to deter speeders it may be possible to achieve the same thing simply by parking empty police cars in strategic places.

Although nudge is an important addition to the armamentarium available to policymakers, it is a rather general conception of a style of intervention, Much of this literature provides interesting examples of how less intrusive mechanisms provide often subtle cues to citizens to behave in certain ways. Can these seemingly subtle interventions be related to the four categories in Hood's NATO scheme? For instance, the example above of the empty police car is actually invoking authority, or the threat of authority. Further, many, if not most, of these interventions depend on nodality and the diffusion of information, assuming a particular reaction of the target individuals based on that information (John, 2013).

As well as having a psychological dimension, policy instruments also can be seen as social and political constructs. The capacity of instruments to achieve their ends may be a function of the manner in which they are perceived by the actors involved, especially by target populations. The nudge mechanisms, and indeed many other informational instruments, tend to rely heavily on accepted social norms for their success. They assume that citizens want to do the right thing, so that if they are reminded what is the right thing to do – pay one's taxes, for example – then they will be more likely to comply. This approach may therefore be effective in societies with common, and publicly regarding, value systems but less effective in more fragmented and individualistic societies.

Evaluating the classifications

The attempts to classify policy instruments have been significant for the development of policy studies in political science, but the multiple versions of classification also raise some analytic questions. What is the relative utility of the various classifications? Are they mutually really that different or are they all looking at some fundamental features of instruments and merely discussing them from slightly different perspectives? Further, does the emphasis on differences in tools mask the important reality that most instruments are really hybrids? Even in those classification schemes focusing on a single dimension, for example, coercion, any individual instrument may have some features that are highly coercive and others that allow a good deal of choice on the part of individual citizens.

The simplest versions of classification of instruments are simple enumerations, for example, Kirschen and to some extent the Salamon's Handbook of Policy Instruments. Simply understanding the range of

instruments available to government, as well as some of the characteristics of those instruments, is not without its uses, especially for a
policymaker thinking about options for a program. That simple enumeration does not, however, provide that policymaker, or the student
of policy, with much guidance about what to expect from any of the
possible choices.

The other classification schemes provide at least some of the needed
answers, but none really links any particular instrument to either a
type of problem or to a likely set of consequences. These classifications
do give us some insight into the ways in which governments can and
do intervene, and emphasize some important analytic points about
the modes of intervention. The classification scheme based on levels
of intrusiveness, for example, forces the policymaker to consider very
carefully the political impacts of instruments, as indeed does the seemingly simple classification used by Salamon. The NATO scheme, with
the amendments from Howlett, does provide some inklings about the
relative utility of different instruments, but is not concerned directly
with their relative utilities.

Choosing instruments

Once we have an understanding of the characteristics of policy instruments, we can begin to consider the ways in which political actors
make choices about instruments. This choice may seem like simply
matching an instrument to the demands of a policymaking situation,
but unfortunately there is no simple algorithm to make the linkage
between the situation and the instrument. Therefore, like most things
in governing, judgment is involved in making those decisions.

Although judgment is certainly involved in the selection of policy
instruments, that statement alone does not go far toward understanding how the choices are made. Further, we should not expect those
choices necessarily to be rational in the usual sense of that term, but
rather they may reflect a number of factors that are more political,
personal and organizational. Indeed, many of the choices will be
made from habit and routine rather than through rational calculation.
Although we are stressing the design of public policies, that design
process will involve a wide range of factors rather than simple answers
for complex questions, Further, those choices are made by individual

decision-makers and by policymaking organizations, with each of these sets of actors bringing their own perspectives to the choices.

Individual decision-makers

Ultimately individuals make decisions about which instruments to use in any situation. Linder and Peters (1989) therefore asked a group of decision-makers in government how they made these choices. Although these respondents provided a variety of answers, their answers could be divided into four groups. The first, and largest, group we labeled "instrumentalists", and these respondents said they would select the same instruments almost regardless of the circumstances. Many of these decision-makers had strong professional backgrounds, so that economists tended to opt for mechanisms depending upon economic incentives, while lawyers depended on law-based instruments such as regulations.

A second group of respondents were labeled "managerialists" (approximately 20 percent of the sample). These actors argued that the selection of instrument was to some extent irrelevant to the success of a program. They believed that they would be able to make any instrument work effectively. As might be expected, the majority of these respondents were trained in public administration, and believed that the management of the instrument was more important than the nature of the instrument itself.

The third group of respondents were those whom we hoped we would find in this research project. These we labeled "Contingentists", meaning their answers were that the choice of instrument depended upon the problem and the situation in which it was to be applied. They possessed, whether from experience or academic training, some sense that tools did indeed have appropriate as well as inappropriate uses and some matching was required. Unfortunately, we found relatively few of these individuals (only 10 percent) in our sample of policymakers. Further, although they understood the potential utility of linking problems and instruments they had only intuitive ideas about how to do that in practice. That said, they hoped to find some means of linking contingencies and policy problems to the choice of instruments.

Finally, there was a small group (5 percent) of respondents, whom we labeled "Constitutivists" who had something of a post-modern, or at least constructivist, conception of instruments and the public policy process more generally. These respondents argued that instruments could not be understood out of the context of the policy problem, and the problem and the instruments to address it had to be constructed simultaneously. This perspective to some extent reflects the complex reality of making policy decisions, but it also tends to make analysis of policy in other than a fully contextualized manner difficult. Further, these respondents may have had, perhaps unwittingly, a perspective on policy similar to that of the "garbage can".

In summary, individuals within public organizations have their individual perspectives on how to design policies, and on which instruments are the best to achieve their policy goals. As well as waiting for opportunities to utilize their favorite policy instruments, individuals – especially the instrumentalists and the contingentists – are likely to be policy entrepreneurs and advocates (Kingdon, 1985 [2003]). As has been argued in the garbage can model of choice (Cohen et al., 1971), solutions chase problems just as much as problems chase solutions. The individuals who have clear ideas about how to solve policy problems are therefore very likely to try to find situations in which they can employ their favorite tools.

Unfortunately, this research did not take into account the manner in which individuals with different perspectives on instruments interact, or the extent to which the organizational framework within which they make those decisions influences their choices. No matter how influential they as individuals may be, they must still function within an organizational setting and the choice of instruments may develop through negotiations among many actors. Therefore, in the next subsection of this chapter we will discuss a range of other factors that may influence the selection of instruments.

Institutions and instrument choice

In the public sector one of the most common explanations for any decision is that institutions are relevant. This is as true for instrument choice as for other decisions, and institutions can have a significant impact on these decisions. In the case of instrument choices, institutions have influences in several ways. The first is that institutions have routines and habits, and they have certain instruments to which they are committed. For example, when social service organizations in most countries are faced with a social policy problem they are likely to think first of social insurance as the most desirable option. These instruments appear to have been effective in the past, so why would they not be in the future?

This selection of instruments through familiarity is not necessarily irrational on the part of organizations. If the organization is familiar with an instrument and knows how to make it function then it is quite sensible to continue to employ it when possible. This logic for selection makes the additional point that instruments do not work automatically but rather have to be administered. And even minimizing decision-making costs when investing in extensive analysis to find the "perfect" instrument is far from irrational. The proceduralists (see above) may be correct and good administration, or administration that is familiar with the dynamics of an instrument, may be capable of overcoming many difficulties resulting from a less than perfect match between instruments and problems. And attempting to train employees to manage a new instrument may be a waste of resources when the familiar instrument may be as effective.

As well as selecting instruments out of habit, institutions may select certain instruments for political reasons, meaning primarily bureaucratic politics. Just as instruments must be administered to be effective, they also have political characteristics that should be considered when being adopted. Emphasizing one type of instrument or another can create a political advantage for an organization. For example, regulatory organizations will benefit if governments attempt to address economic issues through those legal types of instruments rather than through more direct forms of intervention. Or is the best way to address issues of malnutrition through food subsidies (favoring a ministry of agriculture) or through cash transfers to the less affluent families? Either could work but the politics and the political economy of the programs will be very different.

The institutional role in choosing instruments may not be simply a matter of their choice, however, and may be a function of the range of legal opportunities available to institutions. For example, an organization may want to use loans or guaranteed loans as the mechanism for achieving its goals. But to do that it requires the authority to make those loans, or more generally to have access to funds that can be loaned. Of course new legislation could provide the opportunity to make loans, but that is new legislation and therefore involves building a political coalition necessary to enact the law.

Ideas

Ideas can also be the source of choices of policy instruments, as argued by the constructivists mentioned above. We generally think about ideas influencing the substance of policies rather than the instruments for the delivery of those policies, but there are definitely ideas about the relative virtues and vices of different instruments. For example, the neo-liberalism as a seemingly dominant ideology during the 1980s tended to denigrate the direct delivery of public services by governments, producing a spate of schemes for contracting out programs to both market and non-market actors.

Ideas and academic theories provide policymakers with a set of ideas about causation, and these ideas often lead on to a set of mechanisms for intervention. For example, Keynesian economics provides a means of understanding the business cycles that have beset capitalist economies for centuries. If indeed changing levels of effective demand are at the heart of the problem then this understanding leads on to policy instruments that regulate that demand. Likewise, if one accepts the ideas of monetary economics then another set of economic policy instruments become appropriate for addressing the business cycle.

As noted above concerning the "Instrumentalists" in our sample of policymakers the professions also provide their members with a set of ideas about which instruments to utilize. Professional training tends to provide the recipients of that training with a set of ideas about how the policy world is organized and what the most effective means of intervention may be. Professionals may observe the same social or economic problem and not only assume different causes but also have different remedies. While these different ideas at times may be useful, the potential incapacity of participants in the process to understand, much less accept, alternative conceptions of the issues may make effective policymaking difficult.[2]

And it is not only the professions that provide specialized and potentially narrow conceptions of policy problems and solutions. Any group of experts will tend to constitute an "epistemic community" that understands policy problems and solutions through the lens of a body of specialized knowledge, and who tend to exclude others who do not possess this knowledge, or even if they come from a different "school" within the community (see Zito, 2001; Dunlop, 2013). Having this specialized knowledge is of course a virtue but its exclusivity and the restricted vision may not be so virtuous.

Finally, ideas can influence the selection of policy instruments through processes of learning and diffusion (Radaelli, 2009). Although policy diffusion has been in operation for decades if not centuries, the more recent emphasis on "evidence-based policymaking" has made the possibilities of learning about how instruments have worked in other settings more popular with policymakers (Pawson, 2006). The use of the world as a source of ideas for policy does provide opportunities for expanding the range of instruments being used, but also can lead to misunderstandings, and excessive optimism, about the ease with which instruments (or other parts of policy) can be transferred from one setting to another.

Interests

Institutions may affect the choice of policy instruments, but so too can the interplay of social and economic interests.[3] When we think of the role of these interests in policymaking we tend to think of the goals of policy and the structure of benefits being created for members of the society. Interests, usually organized in the form of interest groups, are also concerned with the instruments through which those services are delivered. Instruments can benefit and disadvantage interests just as can the substance of the programs that are being delivered. The effects may be somewhat more subtle than those of expenditures or services, but the effects are still real.

The role of interests in tool selection presents something of a public management paradox. The tools that are the easiest to adopt, meaning primarily that the tools are favored by the affected interests, often are the most difficult to administer, and perhaps also the least effective in the longer run. This can be seen clearly in the Affordable Care Act –"Obamacare". The complex mechanism selected for expanding health insurance in the United States involves the insurance industry directly, and in many ways constitutes a subsidy to that industry. This reduced opposition to the program (at least at the onset) has pro-duced a mechanism that is very complicated and difficult to navigate for citizens.

The role of interests can also be seen in the creation of instruments that are in essence building coalitions among affected groups and beneficiaries. For example, nutrition programs such as SNAP[4] in the United States are in effect serving both farmers and the economically deprived. It might be more efficient simply to give the less affluent citizens a cash transfer and let them buy the food, but the program may not have been adopted without the involvement of the farm lobby. This particular instrument has the additional advantage of controlling the consumption of the poor, reflecting the feelings among conservatives that these individuals cannot be trusted to make the correct decisions when given cash. This instrument thus serves three interest – the needy, farmers and conservative ideologues.

Summary

Trying to understand how policy instruments are chosen involves understanding at least four possible sets of explanations. The first is the role that individuals play, and the various conceptions that policymakers have of the best instruments to match particular circumstances. The second factor is the role of institutions, and especially the dependence on organizations in the public sector on routine and familiarity in the selection of instruments. Third, we can see that policy instruments reflect ideas, including ideas of the professions and other expert bodies with clear ideas about what the best solutions for problems are likely to be. And finally we can see that social and economic interests are concerned with the selection of policy instruments, just as they are with the selection of other aspects of public programs.

While this plethora of possible explanations for instrument choice is generally useful, it also raises the question of which of these explanations is the most effective. The answer, as with so many aspects of policy studies, is that "It depends". For example, a policy that is visible to a number of interests is likely to evoke their involvement and the exercise of their political power in the selection. Likewise, a highly technical policy area is likely to be dominated by ideas and the role of experts in advocating their ideas for the solution will be crucial.

The final and perhaps most important question about tool selection is not really answered by this array of explanations. In a design perspective on instrument selection we want to know how to relate policy problems to the tools that will attempt to solve them. These explanations for choice as yet do not have such a capacity. We can get some inklings from this discussion, for example, that it is not totally irrational to utilize instruments that an organization or individual responsible for intervening in the policy area finds familiar, but there is no algorithm that links problems and instruments with any probability of predicting the most appropriate choice.

Evaluating instruments

Having now enumerated the array of tools available to governments, and discussed some of the politics of choice, we must ask the daunting question: what is a good tool? This question is daunting for several reasons, not least of which is that it requires specifying the situation in which the tool is used before any evaluation can reasonably be made. Further, there are a number of dimensions along which tools can be evaluated, and these are likely to provide contradictory assessments of the utility of the tool, in general and in specific situations. This multiplicity of criteria is a problem for the analysis of public policy in general (see Chapter 7) but is certainly apparent for the assessment of instruments.

In this section I will provide some assessment criteria for instruments coming from economic, political administrative and ethical foundations. To some extent these criteria can be used in a general manner – some instruments are likely to be more efficient than others – but that also have to be understood in context. For example, at times governments may want their interventions into the economy to be relatively invisible, but at other times (crisis, for example) they may want the intervention to be very visible so that citizens will know that it is actively taking measures to address the problem.

These evaluations of instruments are closely related to the evaluations of policies in general that will be discussed in Chapters 7, 8 and 9. To some extent the nature of the instruments involved in a policy will produce the overall effects of the program, although the content of an instrument – the type of tax or the type of regulation – must also be considered. Further, instruments that are preferred by citizens, for example, those that permit greater choice, may make even other unpalatable programs politically acceptable.

Political features of instruments

In the world of government perhaps the first set of criteria that must be considered about policy instruments is their political characteristics.

In government politics generally is trumps so it is important to be able to select instruments that will provoke the least negative reaction from groups in society or from other actors in government. Those two political characteristics, however, may themselves not be the same, and those tools that the general public likes (or is most willing to accept) may not be especially favored by actors within the public sector (political and administrative).

Perhaps most fundamentally the congruence of an instrument changes with the general political and social values of the country.[5] If an instrument does not have such congruence then it is less likely to be effective, and more likely to provoke resistance. For example, market-based instruments are relatively acceptable in the United States but may be less acceptable in European societies that have substantially less devotion to the private sector. Similarly, the United States would find more intrusive instruments involving direct public sector involvement less acceptable while they are normal for much of Europe and Latin America.

The visibility of an instrument often has an effect on its political acceptability. That is, some instruments are readily apparent to the public while others may be well hidden. The contrast between the value-added tax that does not appear as a separate item in the price and the general sales tax in the United States or Canada that is added at the point of sale demonstrates different levels of visibility of a common instrument (a tax on expenditures). For conservatives higher visibility is generally positive, making the costs and effects of government more evident to citizens. On the other hand, liberals (and policymakers) might be more pleased with less visible instruments that might minimize public resistance.

Finally, the accountability of policy instruments is a crucial political criterion. As noted in the preceding chapter and in reference to some extent the discussion above, the use of non-governmental actors and more complex forms of service delivery makes accountability more difficult. Thus, while these instruments and forms of intervention may be less expensive, and in some ways more effective, the difficulties involved in holding the participants accountable for the use of public money and public authority make them potentially suspect politically (Considine, 2002).

Economic features of instruments

Policy instruments have economic characteristics that also must be considered when making decisions about how to design public policies, Perhaps the most obvious of these is the cost of the instrument. Some policy instruments, especially those that involve private actors or "prayers", may impose little costs on the public sector, and in some cases they may be effective in producing the desired outcomes. This then quickly leads on to a discussion of the efficiency of the instrument, with those producing greater ratios of benefits to costs being more desirable even if they involve more total resources (see Chapter 8).

Another important economic characteristic of instruments is the extent to which they tend to distort the market. In the best of all economic worlds instruments (and public sector programs more generally) would not disturb the efficient (sic) functioning of the market in allocating resources. This market distortion can be seen perhaps most easily in tax expenditures such as that given to housing in most political systems (O'Sullivan and Gibb, 2003). These programs tend to divert investment away from potentially more productive uses of the money into the consumption of better and bigger houses than might otherwise be possible. While citizens may like this effect of the policy instrument in supporting home ownership, economists may not be as supportive of this instrument.

Administrative criteria of policy instruments

To be effective policy instruments must be administered, and different instruments are more or less capable of being administered effectively. While the economic costs of the instruments certainly affect their administration, there are other features of instruments that must also be considered. In administering instruments there must be economic efficiency but there are also other conditions that should be met. As in so many other aspects of public policy there are multiple criteria to be considered and there may well be contradictions and conflicts. For example, economic efficiency may be in conflict with desires to target particular segments of the population effectively.

The capacity to target sectors of the population is a crucial administrative criterion of policy instruments (see Ingram and Schneider, 1990; Schneider, 2013). A good policy instrument will deliver the service to those members of the society who are meant to receive it but not to those who do not. This is a difficult standard to meet for any instrument. On the one hand, instruments may deliver the program to those who were not the intended targets, or they may miss individuals or organizations that were intended to receive the benefits or punishments. Conservatives, for example, oppose social programs that may deliver the benefits to individuals who are really not eligible. On the other hand, an instrument that does not identify and vaccinate all potential victims of a dread disease must be considered ineffective even if it costs little per individual vaccinated. Thus, targeting is an administrative criterion but like almost everything else in public policy analysis there is also a political dimension that must be considered.

The enforceability of an instrument, and therefore its effectiveness, is also relevant for its administration. For example, many states in the United States now require citizens to pay the same sales taxes on goods bought on the internet as they would if the products were purchased at a store within the state. The problem is that the states have no reasonable means of monitoring those purchases and as yet have not been able to get national legislation to force on-line merchants to collect the tax for them. Therefore this tax is rarely paid, and may make the state government appear ineffective.

The lack of enforcement of poorly designed or conceptualized pieces of legislation not only has short-term policy consequences but may have longer-term consequences for citizens' respect for government. If governments persist in passing laws that cannot be enforced then it exacerbates the image held by many citizens that it is ineffective and rather inept. That image will, in turn, make the enforcement of even more reasonable laws more difficult. There is increasing evidence that governments are now legitimated as much through their effectiveness as through procedural mechanisms such as voting (Gilley, 2009) so government should be cautious about undermining the perception (and the reality) of its enforcement capacity.

Time plays an important role in the assessment of instruments and their administration. All political leaders would like to create benefits immediately, and deter costs as long as possible. That ideal world is probably not accessible, but policymakers do need to consider time not only for its potential political benefits and costs. Programs that produce their intended benefits quickly are more likely to be welcomed than those that may produce even greater benefits further in the future.[6] And it is not just politicians who prefer benefits in the short run. Citizens also prefer immediate benefits and have a very high discount rate for benefits produced in the future (Frederick et al., 2002).

While some of the administrative impact of time may be political and/or psychological, there may be more tangible factors to consider as well. The world, and perhaps especially the world of policymaking, is uncertain and changing. Therefore the social and political conditions on which a program is premised may disappear quickly, whether through economic crisis, changes in government or through technological change. While immediate benefits are too much to be hoped for, designing programs for a very long-term payoff may be both politically and administratively risky.[7]

Finally, as already discussed, the familiarity of an implementing organization or individuals with an instrument must be considered when designing programs. An instrument that is familiar to the implementers, even if those implementers are ordinary citizens, is more likely to be successful than more creative forms of intervention. Over time the implementer will learn about how to manage a new instrument and the virtues of familiarity will be restored, but the transaction costs are potentially substantial.

Ethical criteria

Finally, instruments affect other values in society than just the utilitarian values captured in the economic assessment. Most of our discussion of policies and policy instruments calculates the costs and benefits and then compares those two totals. But the tools also raise normative and ethical questions that need to be included in an overall assessment of the tools. While there are a number of criteria of this sort, the following provides some insights into the possible impacts of tool selection.

The most important of the values affected by the selection of tools is the extent to which the autonomy of individuals is preserved. We can assume that all else being equal policies, and the tools used to implement them, should maintain the autonomy of individuals. In democratic societies we assume that individual citizens should be able to make as many decisions as possible about their own lives. For example, pensions for the elderly are paid in cash and the recipients can do anything they want with that money. Most pension recipients will use that money for food, heating and all the other necessities of life, although there is nothing to prevent them spending it on alcohol, gambling and tobacco. The state could force pensioners to live in supervised housing and eat three healthy meals each day, but instead lets adults make their own decisions.

The administrative criterion of targeting mentioned already should be related directly to an ethical requirement of equity. That is, in an ethical framework for policymaking individuals who are similarly situated in regards to the targets of the program, for example, who are equally in poverty, should be treated equally by public programs. But an instrument that depends heavily on the individual initiative of the potential recipients for receiving benefits is likely to miss individuals who are illiterate, lack transportation or who are simply shy. Depending upon the individual to apply for the benefit may be conceptualized as a reasonable rationing method administratively but it does violate a sense of equitable treatment of citizens.

The role of administration in producing equity can also be considered from the perspective of the discretion being exercised by the public servants (and non-governmental actors) in the implementation of a program. Programs that provide their civil servants – especially street-level bureaucrats – with a great deal of discretion are less likely to produce the equitable outcomes that are desired on ethical (and legal) grounds. The reforms of the public sector under the rubric of New Public Management have emphasized granting civil servants greater autonomy and discretion, so that the possibilities of these outcomes are increased.

Summary

I have now presented four alternative dimensions along which to evaluate policy instruments. These criteria range from the seemingly hard-headed economic analysis of costs and benefits to much softer and less quantifiable criteria such as normative and ethical standards. Each of these sets of criteria is important and has relevance for the success of public programs, but there are internal differences within each of them. For example, some economic criteria may conflict with each other, so that total costs may have to be considered along with the relative costs and benefits of the instrument.

As well as the conflicts within the four broad categories of criteria, there may more likely be conflicts across those categories. As already noted, the utilitarian nature of economic criteria are likely to conflict with other criteria based more on equity. The difficulty in all these criteria, and the conflicts among them, is that there is no clear way in which to rank and to weight these criteria in designing programs. When faced with choices among instruments the decision-maker must exercise judgment about the relative virtues of the instruments. The criteria will therefore be applied differently in different situations and by different organizations. This judgment is perhaps inevitable and having this list of criteria may help by at least making the choices more apparent to those decision-makers.

The Swiss army knife of government

Roderick Macdonald (2005) has provided one of the most interesting examinations of the tools literature in policy studies, likening the tools available to government to a Swiss army knife, containing an often dizzying array of possibilities. Those possibilities themselves, however, present a problem of choice for governments. Indeed, simply knowing that all these possibilities exist raises the question of what to do with them, and in what circumstances. And even with the several dozen tools on the largest of the knives (or the largest tool chests of any government organization) the right tool may not be there.

Macdonald's full paper provides a number of insights into the nature and selection of policy tools, but several points of the analysis stand out and can serve as a useful summary for this chapter. The first point is there is rarely if ever a single best response (tool choice) for a situation. That selection is cultural and situational and the effects of tool choice may only be understood as the program is being implemented. Therefore, we should perhaps consider that tools that can have multiple uses (the hook disgorger) as opposed to a single use (the corkscrew) are potentially more valuable.

A second point worth remembering in tool selection is that policymakers are not writing on a tabula rasa but rather are intervening after any number of other previous attempts to solve a problem (see Hogwood and Peters, 1983). This persistence of responses means in part that there are preconceptions about what tools are useful and how they should be administered that may be difficult to overcome. Just as the makers of the Swiss army knife have assumptions about which tools we need and how we will use them, so too do organizations in government fall back on their comfortable routines when they select and implement policy instruments.

Third, there is a danger that the availability of multiple tools overwhelms judgment. The more sophisticated the tools of government become, the less room there may be for public servants and other implementers of the programs to adapt and adjust the programs as conditions change or unforeseen circumstances arise. In short, overly detailed instrument choice may in the long run produce rigid and ineffective implementation, whereas a simpler tool (the knife blade?) may have generated just as much positive output with less cost. But how do we know what the limitations of the knife blade may be, even if it is our favorite instrument?

I do not want to belabor the point about the Swiss army knife but the analogy to government instruments is interesting and does help to illustrate some of the dimensions of choice that are involved in designing public policy. Instrument choice appears as easy as reaching into a knapsack, pulling out the knife and then choosing the obvious instrument for the task. But the obvious instrument may not really be the best, even if we were able to define "best" in any unambiguous manner. Further, the particular set of instruments that are most available may not be the best, or even adequate, to achieve the tasks.

Summary

Instruments are crucial for implementing public policies. They sometimes tend to be considered as things unto themselves, but they are primarily means of delivering public programs. Therefore, the successful program designer must consider carefully the match between the goals of the program and the availability of instruments. The best tool may involve treasure, but in the midst of a government financial crisis the only real alternative may be information. So then how do we make information work in that context?

And not only is the temporal context important, so too is the cultural and social context. Understanding the norms and values of the society into which a program is being implemented is important not only for the success of the particular policy but also the general political success of the political system. Using coercive instruments in societies that value autonomy and individual choice may ultimately generate compliance, but at some cost. The skillful designer must always remember that he or she is functioning in a political environment that will influence success and failure.

NOTES

1 For Europe see Héritier and Rhodes (2012) for a similar analysis of contemporary policy instruments.

2 The logic of reframing (see Chapter 4) attempts to address these divergent views and produce effective responses.

3 Of course, institutions also have an interest in their preservation and in minimizing disruption to their established routines. These may not be as visible as the interests of social groups, but they are interests nonetheless.

4 Supplemental Nutrition Assistance Program – the program that used to be called Food Stamps.

5 On congruence theory see Eckstein (1980).

6 The logic of discounting in cost-benefit analysis places this criterion in a more economic context. See Chapter 8.

7 The perception of time in policy may also be a cultural factor, with some societies having a longer-term perspective and being more willing to undergo short-term deprivations for that future gain.

PART III

Evaluating policy

7 Evaluating public policy: an introduction

After governments formulate and implement policies, those policies must be evaluated. The need for evaluation arises from at least two demands about action in the public sector. The first of these is the need to assess how well programs are performing in order to make that performance better (Pollitt, 2013). While the usual image among the public is that government programs do not work very well, the evidence from many countries is more positive (Schwartz, 1987; McConnell, 2010; Baggott, 2012). Even then, however, for programs that are performing reasonably well there is still an opportunity to learn from past interventions in order to improve those programs.

As we will point out below that assessment of performance can be done in a variety of ways. As well as the distinction between economic and ethical evaluations of policy, there is a difference between short-term and longer-term assessments of policies. Much of the contemporary emphasis on performance measurement and management tends to emphasize shorter-term assessments as contrasted to conventional evaluation research (Rossi et al., 2004; Vedung, 2007) that emphasizes longer-term and more fundamental evaluations of programs. These styles of evaluation serve different purposes, and reflect different political priorities, but both can make contributions to understanding public policies.

The assessment of performance is the principal component of this fundamental purpose of evaluation and this analysis can provide opportunities for learning. If we know a program does not work as intended then that information can be used to determine what works in public programs (see Marier, 2013). In addition, the information coming from evaluations can be shared across countries or levels of government, contributing to the "evidence-based policymaking" that has become popular among decision-makers in the public sector (Pawson, 2006). Although there are multiple barriers to effective learning from evaluations, these studies provide a foundation for understanding how and why programs work and also what can be done to improve them.

The second use of evaluation is for purposes of accountability. Holding government accountable for its actions is a fundamental value for democracies, and even for non-democratic governments (Hadenius and Toerell, 2007). In order to know if the remainder of the political system (especially the public bureaucracy) is delivering the programs having been formulated and resourced by the political actors in the system, those services must be evaluated. As well as identifying success and failure of the program, evaluation may also be used to identify the sources of any failures in the system.

The accountability dimension of policy evaluation is especially important given how much of accountability is conducted almost exclusively as a political exercise. That is, instruments of accountability such as question time in parliament are used to embarrass a government, often over rather trivial matters, while major policy issues are shunted aside. These more political forms of accountability make good fodder for the media but may not address underlying public problems. Therefore, emphasizing the role of evaluation in accountability, even in the diminished form of performance management (Peters, 2007), may improve performance in the public sector.

The process of evaluation

The Swedish scholar Evert Vedung is one of the leading experts in policy evaluation. He has argued (2013) that there are intellectually, and in practice, six models of evaluation. Each of these models has a set of governing assumptions that direct the evaluator to examine a set of outcomes and processes that require assessment, and which also raise different questions about those outcomes. While the goal attainment model Vedung discusses is almost certainly the typical model for evaluation, the other models also provide insight into evaluation as a technical exercise and perhaps more importantly as a political exercise.

What Vedung refers to as the "goal attainment model" is the default option for policy evaluation. The basic question for this model is whether the outputs intended by the framers of the program were produced or not, and to what extent, and at what cost. While this model appears quite fundamental, it still depends heavily on the capacity to measure goal attainment effectively. And it also depends heavily on the capacity to identify program goals in some unambiguous manner while, as already noted for implementation, that can be very difficult, and then to identify the extent to which programs have been able to attain those goals.

A second model of evaluation has been referred to by Vedung as the "side-effects model". This model begins with some of the questions of the first model but then expands the scope of coverage of the analysis (Merton, 1936; see below). The question in this model then becomes not only whether the stated goals of the program are attained but also if there were negative side-effects that would undermine the overall efficacy of the program. The difficulty with the side-effects model then is how much negative side-effect offsets how much positive goal attainment? And again, there are the fundamental questions about measurement that must be extended to include negative side-effects, and perhaps also positive side-effects.

"Relevance" is the third model discussed by Vedung. In this model the target of the evaluation is not goal attainment of any particular program, but rather the effects on the underlying problem in the policy area. In the default goal attainment model the assessment is of reaching the stated targets of the program, but in this model the question is whether the underlying social or economic problem is being addressed successfully. For example, a medical program may reach its stated targets but not be very effective in actually improving health.[1] Using this model makes the assessment of a policy intervention all the more difficult, given that it is not always clear what that problem is that is being addressed by the program (see Chapter 2) and the extent to which the program may contribute to overall social well-being.

At one point in the development of program evaluation there was a movement for "goal-free evaluation" (Scriven, 1991). The logic of this form of evaluation is that evaluators should not be told what the formal and explicit goals of the program are but rather should attempt to assess the benefits and the costs of the program in the abstract. Thus, even if the program may be reaching some stated goal its general outcomes for the society, as in the relevance model, may be insufficient to consider it a success.

A fourth version of evaluation, the "client model", permits the clients of a program to make their own evaluations of that program. The previous models of evaluation have been largely objective, depending upon measuring the attainment of goals, or perhaps effects on some underlying policy problem. In this model, however, the question becomes whether the targets of the program are satisfied with the results, and perhaps also if they are satisfied with the manner in which the program is being delivered.

It is quite possible that the objective and the subjective dimensions of evaluation will not correspond (see Bovens et al., 2000). Both forms of evaluation have their difficulties. The objective forms of measurement may be driven by professional and political standards, which are important but may not really satisfy the clients of the programs. Indeed, for some programs that are controlled politically, for example, social welfare controlled by conservative governments, the evaluations may be almost inherently related negatively. On the other hand, if regulated industries evaluate a program positively it may not be accomplishing its goals.

The "stakeholder model" is to some extent the client model writ large. That is, instead of just considering the views of the clients alone, this model considers the views and interests of a whole range of actors connected to, and affected by, the program (Vedung, 2010). The stakeholder model of evaluation is more participatory than the others, and therefore provides a range of alternative perceptions of the performance of the program. At the same time, however, the multiple assessors involved only exaggerates the underlying problem of obtaining something approaching the unambiguous answers about performance that is inherent in policy evaluation.

This model can be expanded even further to think of generalized public involvement in evaluation. Democratic governments have used mechanisms such as public hearings and open public meetings as means of evaluation and policy formulation for some years, but the drive for public participation in these systems has expanded opportunities (Bingham et al., 2005). Increased public involvement has definite political advantages but may not be able to provide the detailed assessment of performance that is desirable for evaluation.

Finally, a "collegial model" of evaluation allows the actors involved in the delivery of the service to evaluate themselves. While this would appear to violate an assumption that evaluation should be done by some independent organization or actor, there are some good reasons to consider this internal model of evaluation. The most important is that who would know better how the program functions and what the potential sources of failure are than the people actually involved. Further, this style of evaluation may be less disruptive to the organization than the uncertainty created by an external evaluation. Finally, this form of internal evaluation has become one component of the general move toward empowering workers within public sector organizations, with the belief that this empowerment will ultimately improve performance (Denhardt and Denhardt, 2007).

These six models can all provide insights into the performance of public programs, and all can be justified as valid means of understanding how government works. Therefore, strategic questions arise concerning which model is appropriate for which settings, and how governments (and their partners) should choose among them. The answers to those questions may depend in part upon the design of the programs and the intentions of the formulators. For example, if a program is intended to be a relatively technical intervention into a well-known policy area then the goal attainment model appears appropriate. If, however, the program has a broader perspective and affects numerous actors in society then the client or the stakeholder model may provide more useful information.

The vast majority of the discussion of policy evaluation focuses on the assessment of individual programs. This is understandable and reflects the need for program managers, and their political sponsors, to understand better how the program is performing. That said, however, there is some need to consider policies in a broader perspective and to understand their interactions. For example, attempting to understand whether a single health program works may also involve understanding how it fits with a range of other health programs, as well as with nutrition, recreation and housing programs. Even more broadly, subjective evaluations of well-being by citizens can be used as a comprehensive measure of the success of public governance (Bache, 2013).

Barriers to effective evaluation

Vedung's discussion of evaluation models above makes it clear that performing effective evaluations is not easy, and involves a number of elements that must be aligned, or even whole alternative conceptions of what the evaluation should be. There are, in addition, a number of specific problems that confound the evaluator, most of these reflecting problems in measuring the effects of programs. Paradoxically, the more meaningful the intended measure, the less likely it is to be reliable and valid. In particular, governments and citizens want to know the ultimate impact of programs on the society and economy, rather than the measurement of outputs such as expenditures or outcomes, for example, the number of services being delivered.

Attempts to measure impacts, which in general occur in the future, and often the distant future, lead to thinking about some specific problems with measuring across time. For example, there are "sleeper effects", meaning that programs that appear to produce little or no effects in the short term may produce significant benefits in the longer term (Salamon, 1979). On the other hand, the initial effects of programs may "decay", so that programs that appear effective in the short term may not have any sustained effects.[2] Unfortunately for policymakers they must make and evaluate decisions in the present, so must estimate what the longer-term consequences of their actions may be.

The above discussion is based on the assumption, often incorrect, that the goals of the program are clearly stated, or even identifiable. The political process is such that it tends to produce legislation, and therefore programs, that have vague or even contradictory goals. Therefore, evaluators may have little meaningful guidance about what to measure, and what outcomes would indicate success. The evaluators therefore may have to make their own decisions about whether to assess what they consider to be the "relevance" model (see above) or to posit more proximate goals and associated measures.

Another problem often encountered in evaluation research is that even seemingly successful programs produce side-effects and unintended consequences. For example, creating the Interstate Highway System in the United States did facilitate automobile travel but also made it easier for people to commute into the cities for work, and therefore made it easier to move out of the cities. Thus, some portion of the decline of inner cities can be attributed to the development of an improved highway system. Further, the greater ease of travel on these highways produced more miles driven with more pollution and more energy imported. Was this program really a success, and if so, to what extent?

Sam Sieber (1980) developed a classification of the unintended consequences of public programs, using the terms "fatal remedies" and "regressive interventions" for the most serious cases that produced results exactly the opposite of those intended. For example, studies of manpower training programs have shown that in some instances individuals who spent the greatest time in the program were less likely to gain employment. In many cases these were individuals who required more training, but in many cases potential employers had the perception that they were difficult cases because they had spent so much time training. Even here, however, it is difficult to call the program a complete failure because many trainees who spent less time in the program were successful in getting jobs.

There are numerous barriers to effective evaluation but one that is not discussed adequately is the role of the intended recipients of the evaluation – typically political leaders and/or the general public. The literature on policy advice has emphasized the need to equip political leaders with the capacity to absorb and assess the advice they are being given (Landry et al., 2003). The information coming from evaluations also must be understood by policymakers so that they use that information for a subsequent round of policymaking. And ordinary citizens may need to be able to understand the evaluations as well if they are to be capable of holding their governments accountable.

Performance management as an alternative to evaluation

The performance management models discussed by Vedung are all based on a conception of evaluation that involves relatively detailed and systematic research to generate answers about the underlying features of programs and government policy. This is expensive and time-consuming for the public sector, and often provides answers only after the program has been operating for some time. In political environments that are increasingly concerned with short-term results and sound bites rather than more detailed explanations of programs, that style of evaluation is increasingly unpopular. Further, as government resources are perceived to be more scarce, governments find that reducing evaluation costs saves money without reducing public services (although of course that may reduce quality).

In part as a function of the spread of the New Public Management, performance measurement and management has become a replacement for evaluation research (Radin, 2006; Van Dooren et al., 2010).

Although this managerial instrument shares a common purpose of assessing what is happening in the public sector, it is also significantly different from evaluation research. Most fundamentally performance management is a short-term perspective on performance, being conducted every three or six months in most cases. While this may provide some immediate feedback for administrators and politicians, the emphasis on producing demonstrable benefits in a short period may undermine longer-term success.

Following from the point above, the emphasis of performance management is on just that – management. The assumption, implicit or explicit, is that if a program is managed well it will be successful in producing the types of results intended. This approach therefore addresses only indirectly the extent to which the initial design of a program is adequate and may permit it to achieve those goals. There is little doubt that good management can contribute to the achievement of goals, but there is also little doubt that the best management available cannot overcome faulty formulation.

Further, even if the program is designed well and still fails, is it necessarily fair, or productive in the long run, to place all the blame for that failure on the management of the organization delivering the program? Clearly managers bear some responsibility for any failures, but there may be other elements within the organization, and in the relationships with other programs and non-governmental actors, that prevent program success. From this perspective performance management can be an exceedingly blunt instrument for assessing public programs and their success or failure.

Finally, the short-term focus of the program also enables managers to "game" the outcomes and to undermine the exercise. Measurement is an Achilles heel of performance management (see Bouckaert and Peters, 2002) and permits managers to engage in strategies that will enhance the appearance, if not the reality, of their performance. For example, a training organization may only accept clients who are well educated and well motivated rather than attempting to train those potential clients who require the greatest assistance. This makes the program look good while actually defeating its purpose.

Crime statistics and police performance statistics provides an excellent example of the problems with gaming performance information. Police officials could classify crimes as lesser offences to make it appear that more serious crime was declining. They would also bargain with criminals, getting them to accept blame for crimes other than those for which they had been apprehended in exchange for lighter sentences – so-called "nodding". This increased the clearance rate of the local police and made them appear more efficient. Officials in local police forces blamed these tactics on the extreme pressures to meet performance targets (see Rawlinson, 2013).

Thus, although measurement is an inherent problem for evaluation, it may be even more so for performance management. There are the same questions about the capacity to measure outcomes and impacts of public programs, and link changes to specific features of a program, and the short-term nature of performance measurement makes that linkage even more difficult. Further, although there is some external monitoring, a good deal of performance management is done through the organization administering the program. This characteristic of performance management is analogous to the collegial model of evaluation discussed above, and may further compromise the objectivity of performance management.

Leaving aside the problems with measurement of performance evaluation, just as we discussed above, these measures can still provide an important starting point for understanding performaance, perhaps especially for the public. Performance indicators in a number of policy areas such as education and health are being distributed publicly, enabling citizens to assess the quality of the schools that their children attend or the hospitals where they may go for surgery. These indicators may be imperfect when compared against some absolute scale of measurement, but may still be useful for citizens attempting to compare different service providers.

In many ways the results of performance management are more useful for consumers than they are within government. In particular, much of the literature assumes that in the best of all worlds performance information will be linked to the budget, but how? If an organization performs poorly should it be punished and lose budget funds, or would that merely punish citizens as much as the organization? Or should the organization be given more funds to produce better performance, or would that only reward failure? There are very difficult problems involved in making evaluations and utilizing those evaluations of performance.

Experiments and evaluation

Most policy evaluation has involved conducting research on existing programs and determining the extent to which they achieve their stated goals, and/or the extent to which they satisfy important stakeholder groups (including clients of the program). This style of evaluation research has yielded valuable information about programs and the outcomes they generate for citizens, but also can have significant flaws as social research. In particular, they are implemented with few controls on extraneous factors that may influence findings, and without considering possible alternative forms for providing those services.

The "quasi-experimental" designs characteristic of most evaluation research can be supplemented by more strictly experimental designs that use randomized assignment and control groups to gain a better assessment of the effectiveness of public sector interventions. For example, in the United Kingdom and elsewhere there have been experiments with sentencing convicted criminals, attempting to understand what types of sentences may reduce recidivism (Farrington, 2003). The New Jersey Income Maintenance Experiment in the United States provided evidence about the capacity of patterns of income support to both encourage individuals to find employment and provide adequate support for the family involved (on Canadian experiments see Forget, 2011).

There is a growing body of experimental evidence used in evaluation, and this is slowly becoming the gold standard for evaluation. While the experimental method has many virtues methodologically, there are also some questions that must be raised when used as a means of policy evaluation. The first is the extent to which findings from an experiment will be replicated when a program goes into effect in reality. Individuals will generally know that they are part of an experiment and therefore may behave differently than if they thought the program being implemented was "The Program".[3] Further, there are ethical concerns as to whether it is appropriate not to give a control group the benefit of a program that may in fact benefit them. Similarly, an experiment dealing with real people may lead implementers to avoid the experimental protocol in evaluation in order to do their jobs in what they deem to be the best manner possible.[4]

Evaluation as feedback

In policy terms evaluation is important for improving public policies. Although that policy dimension is central to evaluation, there is also a more political use as feedback into the political system considered more broadly. That is, policymaking it about policy, but it is also about the role of the state in society and its legitimate position within that society. If governments adopt successful policies they will be able to build their legitimacy, which in turn will increase their capacities to make even more effective policies. And the effects of policy may extend to private institutions as well as to the public sector.

Daniel Beland (2010) has discussed six different streams of policy feedback into the state and the policy process. Although some aspects of these six streams may be closely related, there are a range of significant impacts that do need to be considered. The first of these feedbacks is into the state itself. For example, as Beland points out, programs such as Social Security in the United States, and the social programs more generally in European countries, have been useful for building the modern welfare state. And further these programs have encouraged the creation of a host of interest groups that advocate for benefits from the more active state.[5] And indeed the creation of public sector programs has generated analogous programs in the private sector, with private pension schemes developing to supplement the sometimes modest benefits created through the public program.

Perhaps the most familiar of the feedback effects of policy is the lock-in associated with path dependency and historical institutionalism. The logic has been that if a program is successful it creates positive feedback that helps to institutionalize that program and prevent external challenges. The political aspects of lock-in can be reinforced by programs such as pensions that create stocks of benefits based on prior contributions, making reform difficult. Thus, attempting to produce change in programs after periods of success runs up against both political and administrative barriers.

Finally, and to some extent most importantly, feedback from public programs create the ideational foundation for other programs, and further for the role of the state in providing other types of public programs. Again, for Social Security, the idea of security being provided through the public sector provided a foundation for a range of other programs attempting to provide income security for citizens. Other programs, such as guarantees of "full employment" in a number of countries following World War II, created the foundation for a range of other programs supporting employment.

All these versions of feedback to some extent depend upon evaluations of public programs, albeit more political than technical evaluations. More technical evaluations may also be involved in the process as means of justifying the programs and building a foundation for the political assessment of the program. The examples above are largely positive, but the reverse dynamics are also available if programs do fail, or do not live up to popular expectations. Indeed, there may even be forms of negative lock-in in which areas of intervention become defined as virtually impossible for governments to intervene effectively. For example, if "Obamacare" were to fail it might be generations before the American government would be prepared to undertake health care reform again.

Although the majority of the discussion of policymaking has been of formal political institutions and official actors, evaluation reminds us that this is public policy. Therefore, evaluators and political officials need to find means of making evaluation information available through the media or on-line. This feedback to citizens is a crucial aspect of democratic politics, whether it is done through the media or directly by governments. The public may not be interested in all the technical detail from sources like the Government Accountability Office in the United States or Riksrevisionsverket in Sweden, but they do want to know if the schools are performing well and the water is safe to drink. The pursuit of accountability needs to be more than politicians and administrators discussing programs and should allow the public into the conversation.

Evaluation and learning

We noted above that one of the major purposes of evaluation is for policymakers to be able to learn from past mistakes, or even from past successes, in order to be able to make subsequent policies better (Zito and Schout, 2009). Although learning should be a crucial outcome of the evaluation process, actually learning or drawing lessons from policy (see Rose, 1993) is rather difficult. As we have been noting throughout this book the process of making and implementing policies involves numerous variables and numerous actors, so that determining what the lessons of success or failure are is difficult.

Although the difficulties associated with learning are manifest, the contemporary politics of policymaking emphasizes "evidence-based policy" (Pawson, 2006; but see Hammersley, 2013). The assumption is that evidence generated from policy initiatives in one setting can be used to inform decision-making in others. Those difficulties are increased if there is an attempt to transfer the lessons learned in one political or cultural setting and transfer it to another. The extensive literature on policy diffusion (Braun and Gilardi, 2006) points to these difficulties but also demonstrates that with care learning is possible. Longer-term success in learning depends in part on "deutero-learning", or learning about learning (Visser, 2007).

The question of learning about policy raises questions about the utilization of evaluations. There is an optimistic assumption embedded in the evaluation literature that bureaucrats and politicians will read the evaluation reports, learn from them, internalize the findings and improve the policy. As already noted, there are numerous barriers to effective evaluation and many of these depend on the willingness of the actors involved in the process to utilize the information available. All the evaluation and policy advice in the world will be of little utility if the decision-makers involved in policymaking have ideological blinders, or other blinders, that inhibit their use of the information generated.

Conclusions

It should be clear from the above that evaluation is both difficult and necessary for public policymakers. The necessity arises from the need for accountability, as well as from the opportunities to use evaluation research to improve the quality of the programs being delivered. The difficulty arises in that public policies are themselves complex undertakings involving multiple actors as well as equally complex interventions into the economy and society. Therefore determining success and failure is difficult enough, and determining the sources of that success and failure may be even more difficult.

This chapter has raised some of the general issues associated with evaluation, as well as identified the numerous difficulties associated with effective evaluation. The following two chapters will present two alternative directions for evaluation of policies. One, the more commonly used approach, utilizes economic criteria to assess policies. The utilitarian assumptions behind this model are that more is better, and that "more" can be measured in dollars, pounds, euros or whatever. Therefore, if the economic benefits of a program exceed the economic costs then it can be said to be a good program.

The alternative approach to evaluation considers normative criteria for policy, asking non-utilitarian questions about the choices made by governments in the formulation and delivery of public programs. This approach is perhaps less satisfying for policymakers because it provides less clear answers about the success and failure of programs. The normative approach to evaluation may depend upon the particular ethical perspective of the evaluator, or perhaps on the normative priorities of the formulators and the clients of the program. Therefore, the answer to what is good policy is often unclear.

Each of these approaches to evaluation can provide its own answers but those answers may well be contradictory. Policymakers and evaluators therefore may be put into the position of choosing between those two approaches or of finding some means of using the two together. The superior strategy would be to attempt to put the two forms of evaluation together, but that is easier said than done. The standards and even the logic of evaluation are different, but both approaches can provide insights into the quality of policy and its capacity to improve the lives of citizens.

NOTES

1 The Commonwealth Fund (2014), for example, rates the National Health Service in the United Kingdom as the best health care system in the world, although it notes a deficiency in "keeping people alive". This seems a criterion that is more than a little relevant for the evaluation of a health care system.

2 For example, Headstart, a program to prepare children from low-income families for entering kindergarten. The evidence has been that students who have been through this program are equal to their middle-class counterparts.

3 If they do not know that they are part of an experiment there is an ethical issue for government. In most experimental situations participants would have the option not to participate, but cannot do so if they are not informed.

4 For example, an experiment as a means of addressing spousal abuse was undermined (as a research exercise) by the tendency of the police to arrest perpetrators rather than to offer counseling. Not

only is this the usual pattern of intervention for the police but they felt that they needed to protect the women involved.

5 Skocpol (1992) demonstrated how pensions for veterans provided after the American Civil War helped to build demand and support for veterans' organizations.

8 Evaluating public policy: the utilitarian dimension

The conventional mechanism for evaluating public policy is to assess the economic consequences of the programs. That statement does not mean so much attempting to understand the effects of the programs on economic growth, inflation or other macro-economic variables, although those effects may certainly be one component of the evaluation. Rather, the most commonly used approaches to policy evaluation attempt to measure the costs and benefits of programs in economic terms, usually at a more micro-level. The next step is to compare the net total of costs and benefits against not only other programs but also in some absolute terms (Farrow and Zerbe, 2013).

Unlike some of the other forms of evaluation used in the public sector, cost-benefit analysis tends to be prospective rather than retrospective. This method is used to decide ex ante whether a program is worth pursuing or not. Therefore, along with several other issues to be detailed below, there is a very fundamental issue that much of this evaluation is based upon speculation about the real costs and benefits that are likely to accrue in the future. In this approach to policy it is important to estimate not only how much benefit will be created but also when it will be created, with the standard economic assumption that a dollar today is worth more than a dollar next year.

In addition to the inaccuracy that may easily arise in this prospective analysis, this type of analysis may be easier to manipulate in order to produce desired political outcomes. That manipulation need not be dishonest but may arise out of sincere commitments to particular policies and styles of making policy. This ability to manipulate, or perhaps more politely this possible inaccuracy, results in part from attempting to value outcomes that may be difficult to evaluate in market terms, from uncertainties about the timing of the costs and benefits and generalized uncertainties about the future.

The prospective nature of cost-benefit analysis is important because this methodology is used to advise policymakers about what programs to undertake and which to avoid. Most policy advice is inherently prospective, but much of that depends on the experience and judgment of advisors. Cost-benefit analysis and the associated methods (see below) depend more on a specific methodology to provide that prospective information about policy. It may still need to be filtered through the judgment of experienced advisors, but this is a means of providing policymakers with (what appear to be) hard numbers about policy choices.

The logic of cost-benefit analysis

Cost-benefit analysis is based on welfare economics and logic of the consumer surplus. One part of the intellectual justification of cost-benefit analysis and its emphasis on the creation of "more" comes from welfare economics. The initial criterion for choice coming from welfare economics was Pareto optimality (Blaug, 2011). This criterion was that a move (in this case a policy) would be justified if at least one person was benefitted and no one else was harmed. The difficulty was that this is an extremely conservative criterion, given that very few public programs can be implemented without some losses for some citizens – notably taxes. This criterion therefore can be a recipe for doing nothing.

The so-called Kaldor-Hicks criterion for selecting moves (again policies) provides an alternative to the Pareto criterion that is more conducive to action in the public sector. This principle argues that a policy is socially justifiable if it creates sufficient benefits that the winners can compensate the losers, and still have some benefits for themselves. This does not mean that they will provide that compensation, only that they could. Further, this principle is blind as to who the beneficiaries of the policy may be, so that one that creates large benefits for those who are already affluent is as justifiable as one that creates benefits for the poor.

A second fundamental idea underlying cost-benefit analysis is the "consumer's surplus" (Mishan and Quah, 2007). Stated simply, this surplus represents the amount of money a consumer would be willing to pay for a given product, minus the amount he or she must actually pay. Consumers tend to value the first unit of a product or service they receive more highly than the second, and the second more highly than the third: the first quart of milk where there has been none is more valuable than the second. But units of a product are not priced marginally, but sold at an average price, which means increased production will give consumers surplus value. Thus any investment that reduces the cost of the product or service produces a benefit in savings that increases the consumer surplus. The government's investment in a new superhighway that reduces the cost to consumers of driving the same number of miles – in time, in gasoline and in potential loss of life and property – creates a consumer surplus. And as the time, gasoline and lives saved by the new highway may be used for other increased production, the actual savings represent a minimum definition of the social benefits created by the construction of the new highway.

The concept of opportunity costs is also important in understanding cost-benefit analysis. This concept is based on the rather obvious fact that any resource used in one project cannot be used in another. For example, the concrete, steel and labor used to build a superhighway cannot be used to build a new dam. Consequently, all projects must be evaluated against other possible projects to determine the most appropriate way to use resources, especially financial resources. Projects are also compared, implicitly if not explicitly, with taking no action and allowing the money to remain in the hands of individual citizens. Again, the basic idea of getting the most "bang for the buck" is fundamental to understanding cost-benefit analysis.

When identifying and assessing costs and benefits, the analyst must also be concerned with the range of effects of the proposed program and the point at which the analysis disregards effects as being too remote for consideration. This concept is analogous to the concept of standing in courts that gives individuals the right to sue for damages (Whittington and MacRae, 1996).[1] For example, building a municipal waste incinerator in Detroit, Michigan, United States will have pronounced effects in Windsor, Ontario, Canada that must be considered – even though that city is outside the United States. The prevailing air currents may mean that some ash and acid from the incinerator also reaches Norway, but those effects may be so minimal that they can safely be disregarded. This form of analysis requires making judgments about what effects are sufficiently proximate and important to be included in the calculations. That judgment is also to some extent political, so choosing which effects (positive or negative) can determine the viability of a project.

Finally, time is important in evaluating costs and benefits. The costs and benefits of most projects do not occur at once but accrue over a number of years. If a highway is built, it will be serviceable for 50 years and will be financed over 20 years through government bonds. Policymakers must be certain that the long-term costs and benefits, as well as the short-term consequences, are positive. This, of course, requires some estimation of what the future will be like. We may estimate that our new superhighway will be useful for 50 years, but oil shortages may so reduce driving during that period that the real benefits will be much less. Or, conversely, the price of gasoline may increase so much that the savings produced are more valuable than assumed at present. These assumptions about the future must be built into the model of valuation if it is to aid a decision-maker.

In part because of the uncertainty concerning future costs and benefits, and in part because of the general principle that people prefer a dollar today to a dollar next year, the costs and benefits of projects must be converted to present values before useful cost-benefit calculations can be made. That is to say, the benefits that accrue to the society in the future have their value discounted and are consequently worth less than benefits produced in the first year of the project. Costs that occur in future years are likewise valued less than costs that occur in the first few years. Cost-benefit analysis thus appears to favor projects that offer quick payoffs rather than greater long-term benefits but perhaps also higher maintenance and operation costs. Although there may be good logical justification for these biases, they influence the kinds of programs that will be selected, and that has definite social implications, not least for future generations. Other analytic aids for government decision-makers, such as "decision trees", include probabilities of outcomes to cope with the uncertainties of the future, but cost-benefit analysis tends to rely on discounting future costs and benefits.

Measuring costs and benefits

The most fundamental problem in the actual application of cost-benefit analysis, leaving aside the question of the ranking of outcomes, is the measurement of costs and benefits. To do this requires placing many non-economic outcomes on the common measuring rod of money. It is (relatively) easy to assign a monetary value to outcomes such as less energy used when there are better highways or even the time that commuters may save each day from those better roads. It is, however, much more difficult to assign a monetary value to the lives saved because of a safer road or the environmental losses from building that road. But to make the method work we have to be able to assign such values.

The critics of cost-benefit analysis and allied methods have argued that attempting to assign values to non-marketed factors, especially those such as environmental qualities, is "nonsense on stilts" (Self, 1975). By their very nature, it is argued, these items are not marketable and therefore assigning economic values is logically incorrect and tends to provide the illusion of precision.

The above being said, there are several standard ways of thinking about assigning values to seemingly non-economic costs and benefits. One is willingness to pay. How much would the average citizen be willing to pay for living in an area with clean air as opposed to one with high levels of pollution? This method, referred to as "hedonic pricing", can be determined simply by looking at real estate values in different parts of a city, or perhaps in roughly comparable cities with different levels of pollution. Awards made by courts for loss of amenity values and damages also provide a measure of the value of environmental damage. Finally, these prices can be determined through surveys, asking respondents what they might be willing to pay for public goods such as clean air or low levels of noise (Mitchell and Carson, 2013).

Valuing life is perhaps even more difficult, although many common public sector projects do involve both the loss and the preservation of lives. As already noted, building a new road may save lives, but it may also involve the loss of life for some construction workers. What are those lives worth? The courts can also provide a partial answer here, when the legal system permits claims for wrongful death and judges or juries make awards to survivors.[2] Even these methods, as fair as they are intended to be, appear to many to represent rather heartless choices. That said, as we will point out in the following chapter, simply saying that preserving life is an absolute value tends to vastly oversimplify the difficult choices that must be made when designing public policies.

Problems in cost-benefit analysis

Although cost-benefit analysis is the standard means of evaluating public policies, it is not without its problems. In addition to the technical issues already mentioned, there are more fundamental issues with this methodology. Indeed, for some critics the utilitarian logic at the heart of this model is itself a problem, given that this logical foundation tends to privilege programs with demonstrable economic benefits, and tends to devalue programs that may have less visible benefits.

Following from the above, another of the fundamental issues in this methodology is that the distributional consequences of the programs are largely irrelevant to the evaluation of programs. As already noted, the basic logic of the method is that more is better, but it does not matter who gets the more. Further, when the benefits are produced does matter, and the welfare of future generations may be discounted in this model. Therefore we need to consider some of the basic issues that affect the utility of cost-benefit analysis, despite its appeal on many grounds.

Efficiency as the dominant criterion

Like most economic analyses, cost-benefit analysis relies on efficiency as the dominant goal of policy. The assumption is that society will be better off if programs are efficient and produce greater net benefits for society. While that is certainly an important value, it is by no means the only concern of the public sector and other values need to be weighed against this economic criterion. For example, for some programs effectiveness may be more important than efficiency. The program may be of sufficient concern to citizens to deliver even if it cannot be justified readily on these economic grounds. Analysts may say, for example, that it is cost-effective to close small firehouses in neighborhoods but citizens will rarely accept that economic logic. And equity as a criterion is also crucial for programs being implemented through the public sector.

Although there are numerous criteria that can be applied to public programs, the diffusion of neo-liberalism and its associated programs of the New Public Management have made program efficiency seemingly more acceptable. Whereas cost-benefit analysis focuses on the efficiency of the design of a program, the New Public Management focuses on the efficiency of service delivery. Taken together these approaches to policy and governance do tend to emphasize the one value at the expense of many others when thinking about the public sector.

The discount rate

As noted above, the costs and benefits of programs accrue over time, and there must be some means of placing these on a common measuring rod. To do this both benefits and costs must be discounted to present value. And to do that we need a discount rate – in essence an interest rate – that can be applied to future values. The question then is what rate to apply. The simplest answer is simply to apply the market interest rate existing at the time, treating the public program just as one would any other type of economic activity.

There is also an argument to be made for a social discount rate that is different from the market rate. After all, the public sector is not the market, and there are a range of concerns that may alter the way in which we evaluate future costs and benefits. For example, it could be argued that the appropriate social discount rate should be zero. After all, public benefits are beneficial no matter when they are produced, and reducing them to present value may undervalue them. And imposing market values on public projects may prevent programs that can create some benefits for society from being implemented, especially if those benefits accrue far in the future (see below).

The selection of a discount rate then is both a political as well as an economic activity and it may not be appropriate to permit market logic to dominate the choice (Moore et al., 2004). The zero discount rate mentioned above may make a great deal of social sense even if it certainly does not conform to market logic. There are real opportunity costs for capital that could be used in a public project, and a discount rate that is artificially low may not in the long run produce the greatest benefit for the society.

Inequality

As I noted above, the fundamental logic of cost-benefit analysis is that more is better. There is some logic in that position, given that if there are more resources available in society then all else being equal the society will be better off. But cost-benefit analysis is largely blind to the distribution of the resources being created through the programs it analyses. If all the benefits created in the program are concentrated in a few people, and even a few affluent people, the logic of the evaluation system is that of the Kaldor-Hicks criterion – there is enough that those winners could compensate the losers.

The distributional blindness of cost-benefit analysis is especially unfortunate as a method for assessing public programs. If, as has been argued above, one of the justifications for the intervention of the public sector into the economy and society is to rectify the skewed distributions of income and other assets produced by the market, then certainly the distributional consequences of a program should be considered. Further, although a fairer distribution may be an end in itself it may also have important secondary consequences that could justify its inclusion in the assessment of the impacts of programs.

There are ways in which the distributional consequences might be included in the analysis of a program. For example, if one begins with the assumptions of Keynesian economics that money going to less affluent people will have a higher multiplier because of a higher propensity to consume then some measure of differential economic consequences could be gained. The assumption would be that this higher marginal propensity to consume is indicative of the greater value that the income has to a low-income individual. Rather than being a luxury that can be saved, for a low-income citizen the marginal dollar or euro is important for their livelihood.

Even if the assumed positive benefits of redistribution, or at least more equitable distribution, cannot be measured in this manner it might still be included by monetizing the benefits in the same way as other non-traded goods and services. For example, we know that reducing poverty also tends to reduce crime in a society. We also know that lower levels of poverty tend to be associated with more stable families that in turn is associated with increased probabilities that children will attend school and graduate. Therefore, producing a more equal distribution of income may have real benefits for society as a whole as well as for the individuals who are made better off by the policies.

Inter-generational equity

Most of the discussion of equity and the distribution of benefits focuses on the distribution of benefits across social classes or perhaps geographical regions. There are also important questions of inter-generational equity and externalities (Hepburn, 2007). As already noted, the standard model of cost-benefit analysis discounts future costs and benefits, and therefore emphasizes what happens for the generation that is making the decisions rather than future generations

(Sumalia and Walters, 2005). This model is perhaps good economics but it raises a number of other issues that are important for policy analysis.

The most obvious issue arising is how to protect future generations from a number of negative outcomes from contemporary decisions. Some of those outcomes may be absolutes rather than relative levels of cost and benefit. Depletion of resources such as fossil fuels, for example, may be difficult to cost but has tremendous implications for the well-being of future generations. And climate change implies the extinction of species and perhaps submerging cities or even whole countries. Any attempt to assess outcomes of those magnitudes in simple economic terms would indeed be "nonsense on stilts".

While the potential negative outcomes of contemporary action are perhaps more obvious, there can also be positive outcomes in the future that might be extremely undervalued utilizing a simple economic assessment. For example, investment in research on sustainable energy could produce a bonanza for future generations, with current generations reaping few if any of the benefits of the investment. Again, assessing policies may require more explicit concern about the future, and about successive generations, than is conventionally done when using cost-benefit analysis.

There is ample evidence that most political systems are not good at thinking about the future, and the long-range implications of their policy choices (Jacobs, 2011). This short-term perspective on policy-making is perhaps to be expected in democratic governments, given that political leaders, or at least their parties, want to be re-elected. Bureaucrats have been able to take a longer-term perspective on policy but the increasing use of performance management tends to shorten their time perspective as well.

One of the more interesting approaches to the longer-term implications of policy choices is the "precautionary principle" that has been at the heart of a good deal of European Union policymaking about issues such as GMOs. The logic of this principle, as the name implies, is that decision-makers should exercise caution when adopting programs given that there may be long-term and irreversible implications (O'Riordan and Cameron, 2013). While this principle does indeed take the future into account it may also be a barrier to innovation, requiring some balancing of important principles.

Extensions of cost-benefit analysis

While the basics of cost-benefit analysis are useful for evaluating the utility of policy interventions into the economy and society, there are several extensions of the basic model that also merit some consideration. These methods are all based on the same basic utilitarian logic but apply that logic in somewhat different ways.

Risk-benefit analysis

The framing of cost-benefit analysis is typically in terms of seeming certitude. The costs and benefits are assumed to be identifiable and there is an implicit assumption that they will indeed occur if the program is adopted. The real world of policy, however, is rarely that exact and there are real probabilities of unplanned or unanticipated events. Therefore, in addition to coping with planned interventions and planned outcomes, the unforeseen risks that face any public program need to be considered. For example, when building a dam or a flood control system what level of rain and flooding does an agency plan for? Even if the agency plans for the flood that occurs once every 100 years – a seemingly safe assumption – there is still a real chance of the 500-year flood.

Adding other dimensions of analysis

Cost-benefit analysis is based on economic criteria and fundamental economic assumptions. It is difficult to argue that economic variables are not important for any policy, but it is also difficult to argue that these are the only criteria of relevance. Therefore, there have been suggestions that the methods should be extended to include other important considerations. For example, Simpson and Walker (1987) argued for adding both technical, environmental and risk factors to the analysis to provide a more complete picture of the benefits and costs of programs. These factors would enable the analyst to understand not only the economic impacts of the program but also take into account the risks of other outcomes and especially the impact of the program on the environment.

While adding a range of other factors to the analysis of a possible public program is in many ways appealing, it raises other questions. The first is how does the analyst put together information from these alternative dimensions with the economic results of cost-benefit analysis?

The probabilities are that these different forms of analysis will provide different answers expressed in different terms, leaving the policymaker with the need to exercise his or her judgment. The probabilities are then that the seemingly "hard" answers from cost-benefit analysis will dominate the other forms of analysis and in the end little will have changed.

Regulatory impact analysis

Cost-benefit analysis appears particularly applicable to public programs involving capital investments or other large-scale interventions by government into the private sector. While programs of this nature do have major impacts on the society, there are other forms of public sector activity that also affect the economy and society. While the fundamental logic of analysing these interventions may be the same as cost-benefit analysis the impacts may be more difficult to estimate and may be confined more to the economy and society than to the public sector itself (Arrow, 1996).

Regulatory impact analysis has been implemented in order to assess the effects of public sector regulation. This approach to regulatory accountability was initiated in the Reagan administration in the United States, and then was elaborated by subsequent administrations (Hahn and Sunstein, 2002). This concern with the impacts of regulation has been adopted in a very significant manner by the Organisation for Economic Co-operation and Development (OECD) in a series of regulatory reviews in the member countries (OECD, 2010). These analyses, as well as some by other international organizations, do tend to operate from an assumption that less regulation is better, an assumption that favors businesses but not necessarily citizens or the environment.

Environmental and social impact analysis

Following on from the point above about adding different dimensions to the analysis of policy, there are alternative tools that can be applied to policy choices to supplement, or substitute for, economic analysis. The most commonly used of these alternatives is environmental impact analysis. The National Environmental Protection Act (NEPA), passed in the United States in 1969, mandated that for many federal programs government agencies would have to perform an assessment of the environmental impacts of that project (Taylor, 1984; Jay et al., 2007). The purpose was to attempt to be sure that federal programs conformed to NEPA, and that decision-making was done with an awareness of the impacts of a program – adverse environmental impacts would not necessarily veto a project but the decision-makers did have to justify continuing with the program.

Although the environmental impact statement was an American invention the methodology, or at least the fundamental idea, has been diffused widely. For example, the European Union requires an Environmental Impact Assessment (EIA) or a Strategic Environmental Assessment (SEA) for at least as broad a range of public sector activities as does the US government. This is true for projects funded by the European Union itself as well as for some programs initiated by the member states. Although there are some differences in the details of these assessments as compared to the EIS in the United States the basic idea of some ex ante analysis of programs for their effects on the environment is the same.

Social Impact Analysis (SIA) is an analog of Environmental Impact Statements (EIS) and became part of law soon after the EIS were developed. The purpose of the SIA is to examine the unintended consequences of purposeful interventions, that is, the unanticipated effects of public policies (see above). In particular this method focuses on communities, and on issues of distributive justice in those communities (Interorganizational Committee, 2003). The method also contains a strong emphasis on data collection and analysis in order to provide relatively objective analyses of the effects. And like EIAs this approach has been diffused widely, especially to the European Union.

Summary

Cost-benefit analysis and its various off-shoots are the principal means for assessing ex ante the value of public programs. The methods use an economic logic as the foundation for that assessment, assuming first that "more" is always desirable, and further that everything that governments do can be reduced to a common metric of money. Further, this model of evaluation has a decided preference for benefits produced in the short run and for costs that accrue in the long run.

These basic characteristics of cost-benefit analysis tend to make some programs appear more desirable than others, based on that economic logic. The capacity of this method to give decision-makers a clear answer in pounds and pence, however, gives the method a great deal of appeal for decision-makers as a means of justification as well as an aid to making decisions. As the following chapter will point out, however, there are alternative ways of evaluating policies that need to be considered. These alternatives do not provide the neat answers that cost-benefit analysis does, but they do require decision-makers to think more expansively about the choices they are making in the name of the public.

NOTES

1 R.O. Zerbe, "A place to stand for environmental law and economic analysis", http://www.cserge.ucl.ac.uk/Zerbe.pdf (accessed 8 August 2014).

2 This is, of course, most developed in the United States but in other legal systems there may be administrative rulings that can substitute for judicial decisions.

9 Normative and ethical analysis of policy

The previous chapter has provided one means of deciding on what is a good public policy. This chapter will provide an alternative to the utilitarian logic inherent in the cost-benefit model. Indeed, the search in this chapter is for mechanisms for assessing policies that depend upon ethical standards, but which can still provide decision-makers with usable advice about what decisions to make. One principal virtue of cost-benefit analysis is that it provides those decision-makers with a definitive answer about whether a policy is viable (within the assumptions of that model of course). Unfortunately, the answers coming from the normative analysis will be somewhat more ambiguous.

In this chapter I will present a series of criteria that are important for assessing policies from the normative perspective. The logic of cost-benefit analysis and other utilitarian analyses of policies is that we should assess programs based on "Who Gets What", and the value of those benefits. This chapter will be concerned more with the "logic of appropriateness" of the policies than with the "logic of consequentiality" (March and Olsen, 1989). That is, some decisions about policy may need to be made simply because they are the correct thing to do, regardless of the consequences.

As already implied, there is no clear and agreed upon means of selecting among these various principles, and each does provide a certain important perspective for policy choices. These are all important criteria for making policy choices but they are not necessarily consistent and may even be contradictory. Unlike cost-benefit analysis this form of evaluation does not provide a single bottom-line but rather requires policymakers, and perhaps also citizens, to make judgments of their own about the appropriateness of policy decisions. The various normative criteria that can be applied to policy action could be summarized as the "public interest", but even that criterion requires a great deal of elaboration (Ho, 2011). What follows is a catalog of several of the more important normative criteria for policy choices, as well as discussion of the difficulties in applying these criteria.

Fairness

Perhaps the fundamental normative criterion for public policy is fairness. What the public typically want from their government are policies that are fair, and treat citizens in an equitable manner (Sen, 2009). Citizens may be willing to accept some deprivations, such as higher taxes or loss of services in times of crisis, provided they believe the policy treats all citizens equally, and is being implemented fairly. For example, rates of tax evasion appear lessened if citizens believe that the taxes and their enforcement is fair (Slemrod, 2007). In addition, governments are responsible in the minds of most people for maintaining individual rights and fairness among individuals through law, and doing so through equal enforcement.

While citizens demand fairness from their governments, defining what constitutes fairness is much more difficult. Being human we often think that what benefits us is fair, but programs that benefit other people, and especially people whom we may not particularly like, are not fair. For example, there is a good deal of evidence that people believe that the tax expenditures that benefit them are fair, but others are not (Fancy, 2011). Other people may think that the distributions produced by the market are inherently fair,[1] so that if government intervenes those actions produce unfairness.

If fairness is to be at all useful as a criterion of evaluating public policies it is important to develop some criteria that go well beyond these personal conceptions of fairness. Removing that individual element from the definition of fairness is central to one of the most important standards of justice developed in contemporary political philosophy. John Rawls (1971) developed a conception of justice based on the "veil of ignorance". The central question in this approach is what distribution of benefits and costs would individuals select if they were able to make that choice not knowing where they would actually be in the final distributions of goods and services produced by the market and by government.

The assumption behind the Rawls approach to fairness is that individuals making decisions behind this veil of ignorance would choose more equal distributions than those generally produced by the market. While an individual may enjoy being at the top of such a distribution of goods and services, they in general would be unwilling to take the risk of being at the bottom. Selecting a more equal distribution ensures that the individual would not encounter the risk of being deprived severely. Of course, more risk accepting individuals might be willing to take the chance of "winning big" in the distribution of rewards, but for most citizens avoiding serious deprivation is a preferable alternative.

Of course, we can never really make decisions behind such a veil of ignorance, and governments with complex decision-making processes generally attempt to calculate in advance just who will benefit and who will lose from any policy choice (see Chapter 8). Therefore, while this definition of fairness is an interesting intellectual exercise, it is perhaps not of much utility to practical policymakers. Indeed, much practical politics is about using various forms of political power to shift the burdens of government on to others, and to capture the benefits of government for oneself.[2]

Although the veil of ignorance is a useful intellectual exercise, Rawls has supplied another means of considering fairness in policymaking. Although he ranks equality of opportunity as the primary criterion for achieving justice, his "difference principle" is also closely linked to the pursuit of justice in the public sector (Rawls, 2001). The difference principle argues that in the absence of any other information or criteria, policy choices that minimize differences within the society are preferable. Given the assumption that individuals would choose a more equal set of outcomes in the absence of other information about their own position, pressing for such a distribution of outcomes therefore should be considered fair.

In political terms there are debates about the equality of opportunity as opposed to equality of outcomes. More conservative political regimes, and actors, stress creating opportunities for individuals rather than demanding that all citizens necessarily receive equal benefits in all policy areas. That said, there are some areas of government activity, for example, the enforcement of civil liberties, that do require more strict equality. Thus, saying that fairness and equality are important values for public policy is only the beginning of political debates about the domain of policies to which those values apply, and how more equal societies can be produced (see, for example, Jacobs and Skocpol, 2005).

Autonomy and freedom of choice

As noted above, John Rawls ranked equality of opportunity and the capacity for choice as the most important of the values for justice. He argues that individuals should have the right to be treated as individuals and as adults, and that a just society will provide "fair opportunities" for all citizens. There are always instances in which government must act in loco parentis to protect children and other vulnerable members of society from their own decisions, as well as from others. Political and administrative leaders may also believe that ordinary citizens are incapable of processing complex policy issues and therefore justify a lack of transparency about those issues. And administrators and policy advisors may have some of the same negative evaluations of politicians and feed them only a limited amount of information as decision premises.

The statement from Rawls indicates clearly that one important ethical concern for designing public policies is that individual citizens should be able to make up their own minds about matters that affect their own lives. In some areas that exercise of choice is very easy to permit. For example, citizens do not have to claim their pensions or their unemployment benefits. Most do, but they do not have to. Likewise farmers could choose not to accept payments that subsidize their farms. Even under programs such as "Obamacare" that are considered by many to be impositions, citizens may select one of a number of possible programs of health insurance.

At the same time that there are numerous choices available to citizens, in many other cases those choices will be limited. An individual citizen will be able to select from among a number of health insurance programs under the Affordable Care Act, but he or she will have to make a selection or be fined. Citizens generally cannot avoid (legally) paying their taxes, although the clever use of exemptions and deductions will significantly lessen the obligations (Alm and Togler, 2011). And in time of war citizens may not be able to escape military service.[3]

The ethical, and political, question concerning maximizing individual choice therefore becomes where to draw the line in terms of individual choices versus use of the power of the state to ensure at least minimal consumption of some public programs. For example, while we may allow pension recipients not to accept their monthly payments from government, we become more skeptical when parents refuse benefits for their children. And those parental behaviors become even more suspect when, as in refusing vaccinations, their choices may have societal consequences as well as consequences for the children (Isaacs et al., 2009).

In economic terms the concept of "merit goods" is used to describe goods and services to which individuals or the society should have access regardless of their capacity, or willingness, to pay (Musgrave, 1957). Obvious examples would be public education, nutrition, public health protection and a range of other benefits. That range may depend upon the political and ideological perspectives of the individual preparing it. Similarly, "demerit goods" might be used to describe social and economic outcomes from which members of society should be protected, whether through regulation or prohibition.[4]

Even in the case of merit goods that most of the society assume should be consumed by all citizens, there may still be individual objections. For example, parents may not want to vaccinate their children even though this has value for the society as well as individual children. Should they be allowed not to consume this merit good? Some of the answer may depend on the basis of the objection. Some religious groups that do not believe in vaccination may have an exemption but individuals who have other objections may be forced to vaccinate. The "Hobby Lobby" case in the United States (Burwell v. Hobby Lobby Stores, Inc) on contraception may be the extreme version of the use of these exemptions from law (Carroll, 2014).

The design of public policies may be based on individual autonomy and choice, or it may be more controlling. Some instruments used to deliver public policies restrict the choices of individuals while others permit more choice. At the extreme instruments such as education vouchers permit individual citizens to make choices very much as if they were in a marketplace, albeit with some restrictions such as a mandate that a child must receive some form of approved education. In other policy areas such as safety or public health the instruments used may be "command and control" given the dangers to individuals or the society more broadly.

The increasing use of policy instruments based on "nudges" or other subtle psychological mechanisms (see above; Hausman and Welch, 2010) raises additional questions about individual choice and autonomy. When confronting a command and control policy instrument the citizen is aware that he or she is being coerced, and can react accordingly.[5] When the instrument employed is more manipulative and is largely hidden from the casual observer then the citizen is no less coerced but may have little opportunity to even evaluate the nature of the coercion being applied. Ethically this covert coercion is perhaps even worse than other coercive instruments because it undermines autonomy more completely.

Preservation of life

Preserving life itself is obviously as important as preserving the autonomy of individuals while they are alive (Sunstein, 2013, 2014). We saw above that one of the challenges for cost-benefit analysis is valuing lives so that these extreme consequences of policy choices could be added into the net of costs and benefits of the program. The problem for ethical analysis is in some ways more difficult, given that taking lives has to be justified on some more fundamental moral basis (Glover, 1977), rather than being simply a byproduct of other actions. Likewise, although we tend to consider life as invaluable individuals and governments are constantly making decisions that take lives, or fail to save lives, and we should consider the basis on which those decisions can be justified.

One of the most common reasons that is used to justify taking lives is the preservation of the society. So, members of the armed forces may be asked, or required, to sacrifice their lives in order to preserve their country and their fellow citizens, and policemen and firemen also risk their lives regularly to protect the society as a whole. Likewise, countries have justified the death penalty as a means of preserving society (often with the assumption that this extreme punishment would prevent future violence). Similarly police officers may be sanctioned to use deadly force in the defense of the society, as well as in self-defense.

In some societies taking lives has been justified in terms of maintaining the autonomy of the individual. For example, policies permitting individuals to take their own lives, or permitting physicians to take the lives of terminally ill patients, may be justified on the grounds of autonomy; they permit citizens to make decisions about their own lives (Rachels, 1986; MacMahan, 2006). The precept of maintaining autonomy and the defense of life may obviously be in conflict at times. Laws against suicide, and especially assisted suicide, emphasize the value of life. In other cases such as Terri Schiavo in the United States, government may attempt to preserve life against the explicit requests of the family of an individual who is brain dead (Quill, 2005).

Another common question concerning life versus autonomy concerns using safety devices such as seatbelts or helmets for motorcyclists. Individuals argue that they should have the right to assume the risks of not using those devices, while governments generally attempt to save their lives by mandating their use. In addition to maintaining life and health, government may also justify their impositions through the costs that injuries and death may impose on society, as well as lessening the suffering of family members of those sufficiently reckless to ignore the safety devices available.

Another increasingly important issue posing conflicts between the values of preserving life and individual autonomy concerns the rights of individuals to control the use of their own organs. The general practice in most countries has been that individuals have to sign donor cards of some sort in order for their organs to be available for transplant in case of their death or imminent death (Truog, 2008). The need for organs to preserve life, however, is pushing some governments toward rules that assume that the individual gives consent to using organs unless the individual explicitly opts out.

Another of the most contentious issues in the preservation of life depends upon the definition of when life begins. The intense debate over abortion in any number of countries has pitted those claiming that life begins at conception against those claiming that life only begins with the viability of the fetus (Halliburton, 2014). And these debates may extend to techniques such as in vitro fertilization that are argued to interfere with natural processes. For some participants in the debate, however, these technical details are irrelevant, with the right of a woman to control her own body and reproductive life as paramount values. These values cannot be expressed in the financial values of cost-benefit analysis but depend on more fundamental values.

Maintaining life as a political issue also confronts the conflicting values placed on visible lives and less visible but equally valuable lives. This may appear when a woman's life is threatened by continuing a pregnancy, but may arise even more obviously when a mountain climber is stranded on the side of a remote mountain.[6] Governments will spend significant amounts of money attempting to save that individual, even if he or she got into the position largely by their own volition. The money used in the rescue would, if used to improve highways or for other safety programs, potentially save hundreds of lives. What is the correct use of this money, based on a principle of preserving life?

Although the preservation of life is a fundamental value its application to public policy issues is by no means simple nor unambiguous. This value cannot be considered in isolation from other important values, especially the preservation of individual autonomy. Therefore, decisions about preserving life become clouded with numerous different values involved. It is easy to say that life is absolute and sacred but in reality individuals and governments make decisions that take or threaten life. As with so much of policymaking, the choices being made are complex, contradictory and often incomplete.

Stigma

Equality is one of the underlying principles of fairness, but societies sometimes find maintaining equality difficult. In some societies people may be stigmatized because of race, or religion, or characteristics such as physical deformity or mental illness. But the actions of governments and their public policies may also be the source of stigmatization and poor treatment by the members of society. Almost all citizens in modern governments are the recipients of some form of government benefits. These may be well disguised, as when more affluent citizens receive their benefits in the form of tax expenditures. Although citizens are all beneficiaries, programs are not delivered in ways that are necessarily equal, and the recipients of some programs are treated poorly at the point of delivery, and simply receiving some social benefits may make some citizens appear less deserving, and even less real citizens, in the eyes of the public and especially in the eyes of some political elites.[7]

Being the recipient of means-tested benefits often means that other members of the society will consider the recipients as less worthy because of those benefits. The assumption, especially in societies such as the United States and to some extent the United Kingdom, is that the individual is somehow less capable and worthy of respect than are those who do not receive benefits. There is a long tradition of characterizing the "deserving" and the "undeserving" poor in society (Handler and Hasenfeld, 2006; Erler, 2013), with the elderly and children considered deserving of concern while individuals of working age who are not supporting themselves considered undeserving.

All else being equal, policies should be designed in ways that minimize the stigmatization of the recipients of the benefits. This means primarily not using means-tested programs to deliver social assistance, or if means-tested programs are used they should be administered in ways that do not make the recipients visible to the remainder of society. The problem is that social assistance programs are almost by definition means tested, meaning that designing programs to hit the target population effectively (Schneider and Ingram, 1993) without stigmatization is difficult.

In addition to the stigmatization that may be produced simply by the nature of the program, there may be additional difficulties produced for the beneficiaries of programs through the manner in which they are delivered. A number of studies from a variety of cultures (Dubois, 2010; Auyero, 2012) have demonstrated that the recipients of social programs are not treated as well as customers in the marketplace or the recipients of other public programs. T.H. Marshall (1964) once commented that the welfare state would not be achieved until people standing in line for the dole were treated in the same manner as people standing in line for opera tickets. If that is true, then there is a very long way to go before the type of equality foreseen by Marshall is achieved.

There may be ways of delivering programs to the less affluent, or to any other group that may be stigmatized, without creating that stigma. One mechanism for reducing stigma is through using universal benefits rather than means-tested benefits. One example of a program of this nature is the child benefit used in most European countries (Alesina and Glaser, 2004), with parents[8] of children regardless of their income receiving a monthly allowance. For the more affluent this becomes taxable income while for the less affluent it is a direct benefit. The other option is tax-based programs such the earned-income tax credit (Alstott, 1995) that provides benefits through the tax system, just as many affluent citizens receive benefits through tax expenditures.[9]

Stigma is a particular problem for social assistance programs, but it is part of a more general problem in policy design of labeling. That is, by creating categories within which individual cases are slotted, public policies may create not only stigma but also self-fulfilling prophecies about the behavior of individuals. For example, labeling individuals as "disabled" can create rights for those individuals and at the same time label them as incapable (Bagenstos, 2000). Likewise, placing children in "remedial" classes may provide them with a suitable education but also label them as less capable than their peers, and may reduce the probabilities that they will ever succeed in the educational system.

Thus, stigma is about the formal criteria required to receive benefits, but it is also about the manner in which people are treated by their government, and by their fellow citizens. Governments can remove formal barriers to programs and make them more universal, but at times attempts to assist citizens may produce negative social and psychological outcomes for those citizens. If benefits can be monetized fairly and made universal that is beneficial but governments have difficulties in controlling the often inadvertent behavior of citizens as they relate to other citizens.

Thus, as already noted, the problem of stigma and labeling presents a dilemma for public policy designers. On the one hand, targeting programs to a specific population represents good design, providing a benefit to only those eligible but not wasting resources on those who are not. In doing this, the programs may inadvertently, or perhaps intentionally, stigmatize some groups within the society. Weighing these two criteria for good policy – one administrative and one more ethical – is but one of the numerous challenges confronting policymakers. The policy solution selected is dependent on ideology, culture and politics but those choices will still have to be made and the consequences accepted.

Truth-telling, many hands and dirty hands

Policies may be designed in ways to enhance their fairness and the autonomy of citizens, but they also have to be implemented. The implementation process also involves a number of challenges to an ethical delivery of public policies. Some of the above values, for example, stigma, may in reality be as much a function of the manner in which programs are delivered as they are of the underlying design of the programs. Policy and administration may be treated as separate academic enterprises, but are in reality intertwined, and administration affects the success of programs as well as the impact of programs on citizens.

One of the crucial ethical issues for the delivery of public programs is "dirty hands" (Walzer, 1973; Coady, 2010). Although governments and individual public servants would like to be able to make decisions openly and ethically, there are times at which more difficult choices must be made. The problems of having to act in less than a fully ethical or truthful manner is usually considered to be a particular issue for international politics, as when diplomats must prevaricate on behalf of their country and national security reasons are used to restrict access to information (Thompson, 1999). Even at the domestic level governments must sometimes lie or shade the truth in order to make programs more effective, or perhaps to preserve other important values, including the lives of citizens.

Truth-telling is a fundamental value in most ethical and religious systems (Bok, 1978). Telling the truth is valued for its own sake, but it is also valued for more consequentialist reasons. If one individual does not tell the other the truth, then that second individual will be making decisions with false information and hence may make poor decisions. The first, less than truthful, individual will have exercised power over the second. While this lying may be acceptable in social situations – the familiar little white lies that may facilitate ordinary life – it becomes much more problematic when dealing with public policies.

Even in the public sector there may be instances in which lying may be acceptable, or even necessary. As already noted, in foreign affairs it is generally accepted that diplomats or national leaders may have to lie on behalf of their countries. The argument justifying this is that representatives of one state have obligations of truthfulness to the members of their own society but not necessarily to members of other societies, especially when those societies are in adversarial or even competitive relationships. Thus these officials accept the burden of "dirty hands" by lying, or perhaps by doing even more serious wrongs than lying to others as a consequence of accepting positions of responsibility.

In policymaking secrecy, and a lack of transparency, by not disclosing the full truth may be a form of lying. As with other forms of lying on behalf of one's country, this behavior may be considered justifiable in international affairs, but becomes less viable in domestic politics. The assumption, at least among citizens in democratic regimes, is that their leaders have an obligation to be truthful to the members of their political community. Indeed, the obligation for truthfulness may be greater in government because it represents a collective undertaking for the society and the leaders have duties to the members of the society.

The question then becomes when, if ever, is lying and secrecy justified when dealing with the citizens of one's own country. Given that information on national security issues provided to the public would easily be dispersed to potential adversaries then maintaining secrecy in those areas appears necessary. Likewise, secrecy can be justified for information that could be embarrassing to individual citizens or which might harm individuals economically (patent applications, for example). The assumption is that all other information should be widely available to the public so that they too may be involved in the policy process.

Making government fully transparent may have a strong moral claim, but it may not enhance the quality of the policies being made (see Torfing et al., 2012, chapter 7). Indeed, some countries have tended to shield their policymaking from public view in order to ensure that the process will not be unduly pressured by external forces.[10] If policy advisors are to provide the policymakers with "frank and fearless" advice, then they may require some protections from external scrutiny. This is especially true for civil servants who expect to be able to work anonymously and whose continuing effectiveness in their positions may depend upon protections.

In summary, the value of truth-telling and transparency in government like so many of these other values affecting public policy are difficult to make absolute. These values may be phrased in absolute terms – "Thou Shall Not Bear False Witness" – but in reality there are compromises and even direct denials of those absolutes. The answers to this question are usually phrased in utilitarian terms – the benefits produced for society are greater than if the truth were told. There may be other ways of justifying the choice, such as the preservation of life – but most answers come down to utilitarian reasons. We began this chapter looking for non-utilitarian approaches to evaluating policies, but these appear difficult to maintain once they confront tangible losses for individuals, and especially losses for the society as a whole.

Summary

Governments have to make difficult choices when they make and implement their policies. Even policies that may be effective, and even efficient, in economic terms may entail other social and political effects that may be undesirable. But even if there are attempts to make policy choices congruent with ethical values, the decision-making problem is not over. There are a number of important ethical values that can be contradictory, or at least not consistent. Therefore, policy choices may involve balancing a number of important values and attempting to make a choice that minimizes the adverse effects.

Like the discussion of cost-benefit analysis and allied methods these considerations may be part of the formulation of the policy rather than an ex post evaluation of the success or failure of a program. That said, however, some of the effects of programs on individuals may not become apparent until they are implemented. And given that these programs are being constructed and assessed in a political environment, the choices among values inherent in these decisions will include much more than ethical or philosophical values. In the end political or even economic values may trump ethical concerns as governments attempt to produce a package of ethical and affordable policies.

NOTES

1 These people are, rather naturally, those who benefit from the distributions produced by the market.

2 James Q. Wilson's (1980) analysis of politics focused on the concentration of costs and benefits.

3 In most societies the military draft is a thing of the past but in some countries such as Switzerland and Singapore there is universal military service. In principle, in others a draft could be restored if military personnel requirements increased significantly. See Levi (1997).

4 This concept is very similar to that of externalities discussed previously. In both cases economic or social action produces "bads" that affect other citizens, and the role of government is either to prevent those bads or compensate those who are affected.

5 That reaction generally is to comply with the regulation, but perhaps then to engage in political activity to modify the policy.

6 I have nothing against mountain climbers – this is only an example of risky individual behaviors that have public policy implications.

7 Mitt Romney's famous rant about 47 percent of the population dependent upon government is a now infamous example of stigmatization of citizens who receive public benefits.

8 In most cases the mother is designated as the recipient, assuming she will bear primary responsibility for caring for children.

9 This is one of the few effective social programs that has been primarily an American invention.

10 Much of the justification for the Official Secrets Act in the United Kingdom, and analogs in other

Westminster systems, was to preserve the internal openness of the discussions. The assumption was having to make decisions in public would produce policy choices that were more politically palatable but not so good as policies.

10 Conclusion: policy success and failure

Policymaking is the central activity of government. Governments do not always make and implement policies on their own but rather often involve partners coming from the private sector – both market and non-market actors. No matter who is involved in the policy process, they face serious challenges to reach their policy goals, and their political goals associated with the policy. The design perspective I have adopted in this volume assumes that policymakers attempt to shape programs in ways that can generate success, but achieving that success is a difficult and sometimes impossible process.

But what is success? It has seemed that identifying policy failure has been easier for both citizens and policy analysts. For example, there have been studies of failures in planning (Hall, 1980) and implementation (Pressman and Wildavsky, 1974), as well as more general discussions of "policy fiascoes" (Bovens and 't Hart, 1996). Other works have attempted to contrast success and failure in different national settings and different policy areas (Bovens et al., 2000). Further, there have been several discussions of the failures of specific policy instruments and styles of intervention (Sieber, 1980; Birkland and Waterman, 2008).

The evaluation sections above developed several versions of policy success, but these definitions were perhaps excessively restricted. In particular cost-benefit analysis equates success with policies that produce greater economic benefits than they require in costs. But most cost-benefit analysis is ex ante, and we may not know if even that minimalist goal is achieved for some time. For most citizens the idea of success in public policies is more related to effectiveness than to efficiency, and is generally more concerned that services are actually delivered rather than the relationships to costs.

Process success

Allan McConnell (2010) has provided an extensive discussion of policy success. He argues that this success has three dimensions. The first is the process dimension of policy success, or failure. At the most basic level policymaking processes need to be able to generate policy decisions, and to do so in a timely manner. If we consider the gridlock and the inability of some governments to make decisions, this seemingly simple dimension of success may not be so simple. While we might think of these deadlocked processes as typical of less-developed political systems, the failure of the US federal government to make a budget in most years of the past decade demonstrates that this can be a more generic phenomenon.

As well as simply making decisions, the policymaking process must be able to maintain legitimacy for the political system. Most political systems have clearly defined legal and constitutional procedures for making policy, so any attempt to circumvent those rules may bring the legitimacy of the policy, and the system more generally, into question. This having been said, however, the formal decision-making process may be slow, and some difficult issues may not be easily resolved through processes with numerous veto players (Tsebelis, 2000). Further, non-majoritarian institutions (Majone, 2001, 2002a) may be able to make those difficult decisions that more political institutions cannot.

Program success

Program success represents the second dimension of policy success in McConnell's analysis. This dimension is what most people might think of as policy success more generally, meaning actually reaching the intended goals of the policy. A successful policy in this perspective delivers benefits to the intended targets of the program but, as the evaluation chapters have indicated, ascertaining the extent to which that success has been achieved may not be easy. Although we will discuss political success below, the definition of program success may also be politically defined.

First, there is the question of which goals, and whose goals. Few policies are so simple or so unambiguous that the analyst can say that goals have been reached. For example, is building a new highway about energy efficiency, traffic safety, reducing time lost for commuters or providing jobs for construction workers? The answer is usually that it is about all four. And if the program does well on most goals, but fails on one or more then is this program a success or not? That answer may depend primarily on the organization responsible valuing its core policy goals – reducing commuter time and traffic safety in the case of the highway department – significantly higher than the ancillary goals.

Success and failure of programs may also be affected by unintended consequences of programs. Is a program that reaches its principal goals but also has a number of negative side-effects really a success? Once again this may depend heavily upon who is asked to evaluate the program. And for some analysts any program that is very expensive and is perceived as wasteful may not be considered a success even if it hits the intended targets. Different ideological perspectives also will produce different perspectives on success and failure of programs. For example, for liberals (in the American sense of the term) having more people receive social benefits may be a success, while for conservatives that would be failure.

Political success

The political nature of some of the answers that can be given to the questions above lead rather naturally to the third dimension of success and failure, which is political. Public policymaking is operating in an inherently political environment, and the effects of policies on the political fortunes of the actors involved will, of course, be of great concern for those participants in the process. Perhaps most obviously the impact of policy choices on the electoral fortunes of the participants will be central in the minds of the political class. If, as Anthony Downs (1957) argued some years ago, politicians make policy to be elected rather than vice versa then this is a crucial dimension of success.

But the political dimension of policy success extends well beyond the electoral success of specific politicians. It is becoming increasingly apparent that the legitimacy of political systems depends upon the outputs of the system more than the process by which policies are made (Gilley, 2009). This is especially true for the European Union in which the electoral connections of citizens to much of the leadership is tenuous at best (Scharpf, 2009). But many national states are legitimated by their capacity to maintain economic growth and generous welfare state benefits for the public.

Summary

Policymakers want to be able to say that they have produced effective and successful policies for their societies. But that claim is not as simple as it might appear and policy success and failure is complex and multi-dimensional. Further, success and failure may be perceptual and constructed (see Stone, 2002), and those perceptions differ across individuals. Given that politicians and citizens often have very different perceptions of the political and policy world it is only natural that they will evaluate policies differently.

Obamacare in the United States represents a clear example of this multi-dimensionality and complexity in assessing success and failure. While there is little doubt that the launch of the program was a fiasco, by spring 2014 the program had reached and then exceeded its target for enrolling citizens (Somashekar and Millman, 2014). But there did not appear to be as many young enrollees as hoped, given that younger people with lower health care costs were important for the financial viability of the program. And many Republicans and even independents continued to rail against the program. Is this a success?

Going beyond individual policies

The discussion of policymaking to this point has focused on the success or failure of individual programs, but governments make and implement hundreds, if not thousands, of programs. This crowded policy environment involves a number of policies that conflict with one another, and others that could support one another but do not work together. Therefore, one crucial element for improving the success of policies is to improve their coordination, and to foster more integrated policies across subsystems (Peters, 2014a). In some cases programs may actually contradict one another, as when the US Department of Agriculture supports tobacco farming, while the Department of Health and Human Services discourages smoking.

It is very easy for analysts and practical policymakers to say that there should be more coordination across policies, but producing that coordination is much more difficult. There are a number of organizational and political barriers to producing coordination. At one level the protection of "turf", meaning the budgets, personnel and policy space allocated to an organization in government (Beale, 1995; Blatter, 2003), and the control of information to preserve organizational power hinder coordination. Differences among political parties in government and vertical coordination issues in federalism contribute further to continuing separation and conflict among policies. And finally professionalism, while perhaps contributing to success of individual programs, may also make cooperation with other programs more difficult.

Although governments tend to be divided into a large number of specialized programs, most of the important policy problems facing government are not so specialized. For example, improving the health of the population is a major policy issue but cannot be handled just using the programs within a ministry of health. Improving health also involves food and nutrition programs, sports and recreation, social assistance, education, housing and perhaps other policy areas. Therefore, getting all those programs to work together cooperatively presents a major opportunity for governments, but also a major challenge. This challenge typically is addressed through the hierarchical power of executives or central agencies, but network or even market devices may be effective in producing needed cooperation among organizations and individuals.

Reactions to policy failure: governing in the shadows

We have already argued that market failure is a compelling reason for the intervention of the public sector into the economy and society. Even anti-government conservatives may recognize that markets can be imperfect and some means of compensating for those failures must be found. But even étatiste supporters of government interventions must realize that governments can, and do, also fail to deliver the programs that they have created as effectively as citizens, and most of the program's personnel, would like.

The preceding section of this chapter has demonstrated the difficulty of defining and assessing policy success and failure. When there is a real or perceived failure then there is an impetus for change. Government organizations can learn from their past successes and failures and modify programs during the next round of decision-making, adapting to changes in the environment and the effects of their own interventions. But public programs may in some cases be incapable of actually delivering effective policy, either because of their own weakness or the nature of the policy problem being addressed. What then are the options for policymaking?

Fritz Scharpf famously argued (1997) that when governments delegate to social and market actors that delegation is occurring within a "shadow of hierarchy". This means that governments retain the legal authority to withdraw the delegation whenever the agents fail to act properly. Policymaking is also occurring in a shadow, or indeed a set of shadows, so that when government fails to deliver the policies there are other alternatives. In the contemporary political environment the obvious alternative to the public sector has been the market. Whether through privatization, the use of market-based instruments such as effluent charges or vouchers or contracting to private sector actors markets are a major alternative to public sector provision.

The market is not the only alternative source of policy and service provision for citizens. Social actors such as not-for-profits and faith-based organizations are also alternative sources for policy and policy delivery. These actors are especially important in areas such as social policy and education where these organizations often are major or even dominant actors. Further, with the financial strains in the welfare state as a function of demography and tax resistance (Ferrara and Rhodes, 2013) these social actors are likely to become even more significant as the providers of public services.

Finally, expertise can function as an alternative source of policy. In a number of policy areas such as economic policy, or areas of energy policy, governments may want to delegate to expert organizations such as central banks, regulatory organizations or scientists. These organizations also have the capacity to make "credible commitments" to individuals and firms so that those actors can make long-term decisions (North, 1993). While expertise and credible commitment can be effective in making and delivering public policies, there are also problems for democracy when policy is so dependent upon expertise with little democratic control.

These four alternative sources for policymaking and governance exist in any society, and to some extent exist for any policy area. Simply saying that, however, is only the beginning of understanding the manner in which choices of styles of intervention are made. One may argue that this represents an evolutionary approach to policymaking, but it must also involve agency (Capano, 2009). How do actors involved make decisions about how to move away from rather conventional formats for public policy toward using other actors and institutions in order to provide more effective policymaking? And when will they want to move back to those conventional formats for policymaking?

Not only is there a question of agency and decision-making in the movement among broad approaches to policy expressed here as a set of "shadows", but there is also a question of mixtures. Few policies in contemporary governments can be seen as being delivered purely by one or another institution. Rather, most policy delivery represents hybrid forms of action and interactions among numerous actors (Torfing et al., 2012; see also Chapters 5 and 6). Therefore, policymakers will need to consider the nature of these hybrids and the way in which the multiple actors can combine to provide the most effective public services.

Continuing challenges to studying public policy

Although the study of public policy has made numerous advances since the initial formulation of the policy sciences by Lasswell and his colleagues, there are a number of continuing issues about how best to continue that advance. To some extent the problem in studying public policy is that there is an embarrassment of riches. As several of these chapters have pointed out, there are multiple models of policymaking, and multiple approaches to particular aspects of the policy process such as implementation. While this is a rich analytical palette from which to choose when painting a picture about policy, the problem is choosing under what conditions to employ one approach or another. This question is largely empirical, because there are no metatheories that permit making choices among the available options (see Alexander, 1984).

Although there are many theoretical options for understanding public policy, there are still some significant issues that are not addressed adequately. One may be explaining innovation in policy. There is a large literature on policy change that certainly touches on issues of innovation, but much of that literature has rather incremental assumptions. While that may reflect reality, as indeed much of policy change in governments is incremental, it does not provide an effective understanding of the creation of genuinely new and innovative approaches. Nor do we understand the structures and procedures that could foster greater innovation.

Public policy in a comparative context

The necessity of making choices about policymaking strategies outlined above also points to the need to consider public policy in a comparative context. The discussion in this book has largely been generic, assuming that policymaking is virtually the same everywhere. While that generality is certainly true at one level, there are also important institutional and cultural features of individual policymaking systems that demand more nuanced understandings. These general understandings of policy may be a good place to begin our discussions but they are not always a good place to end them.

The need to think comparatively is at least as true for different policy areas as it is for different political systems. Gary Freeman (1985) has argued that the differences across policy areas are more significant than those across countries, and that health policy (as one example) may be more similar in several countries than education and health within the same country. Factors such as the nature of the interests involved, the level of technical and professional content, the nature of the instruments available and a host of other factors may all differentiate different policy areas and differentiate their politics, as well as more technical aspects of their delivery.

If we consider some of the general models of policymaking above in light of different policy areas some of these differences become apparent. For example, if we consider health policy through the lens of the ACF the shift in emphasis in health policy from more technical, scientific forms to the "science of delivery" (Mulley et al., 2013) can be seen as creating a new vision for health care. Whereas this discussion appears largely to be conducted on the basis of science, proposed shifts in policy areas such as education or social policy have tended to be more politicized. Similarly, the scientific nature of health policy and energy policy may be less amenable to the multiple streams approach than other policy areas with less clearly defined foundations.

Leaving aside comparisons among policy areas, there are also important comparisons across political systems that influence policy and policymaking. For example, the complexity of policymaking systems, defined perhaps as the number of veto players in the system, will influence the capacity to make effective policy decisions. Weaver and Rockman (1993) assessed the capacities of parliamentary versus more complex presidential systems to make policy choices, finding no clearly defined differences. Scharpf (1988), on the other hand, argued that systems with multiple veto players, such as the European Union, find it difficult to make other than minor adjustments from the status quo. The multiple checks and balances in American government also inhibit effective policymaking, especially when complicated by sharp ideological differences between the political parties.

The above being said, complex political systems may also be able to foster innovation, or at least provide openings for innovation. Federal systems, for example, allow innovation in sub-national units that might be difficult or impossible at the central government level. And systems with multiple active policymaking institutions, including perhaps an active court system, will provide more loci for action than would more linear parliamentary systems. Thus, while polycentric political systems may find it difficult to be decisive, they may have broader policy agendas that ultimately will produce more innovative programs.

As well as structural differences across regimes, there are also important cultural differences. One classic example of these differences may be in Esping-Andersen's (1990) discussion of types of welfare states. Despite the numerous critiques of this work (see Hemerijck, 2012), it does demonstrate the manner in which social and cultural factors influence policy choices. These cultural influences are often quite subtle, and may lead to stereotyping, but they are real. And they may be more difficult to change than policy regimes based more on political or ideological foundations.

As implied above, the difficulty in comparative analysis of public policy may be in making causal links between presumed independent variables and policy choices. And further, making the link between those independent variables and the success and failure of programs. Policymaking is complex and involves numerous decisions. As Pressman and Wildavsky (1974) pointed out, even the implementation stage of the process may involve a hundred or more independent decisions. Therefore, attempting to track the process and determine when and how certain factors influenced final choices is at best difficult. This is especially true when attempting to understand these choices in a comparative context.

We are therefore left with what may be another paradox for studying public policy. On the one hand, understanding the dynamics of policy, and perhaps even its content, is best done comparatively; without the comparative framing of policy outcomes it is difficult to understand their broader relevance. On the other hand, however, that comparative frame introduces an even greater array of factors that can influence the outcomes, so that explanations may become more convoluted and more difficult to understand.

As much as I favor comparative analysis for developing more nuanced understandings of policy, bringing in the comparative dimension may pose extremely difficult challenges, and those challenges may not be worth surmounting for decision-makers faced with an immediate problem within their own context. Comparative analysis may introduce some factors for explanation that while useful for the explanation may not be manipulable by those decision-makers. While we are interested in public policy for scientific reasons, we are also interested for more practical reasons – we want to be able to make and implement better policies. Given that practical concern, having explanatory variables that can be manipulated readily enables the policy analyst to provide useful advice to decision-makers.

Linking with institutions

Much of policy analysis appears to be almost institution free. Although mentioning numerous actors, mostly the bureaucracy, the models of the policy process tend to assume that those institutions are rather uniform across countries, and therefore the models developed in one setting will be applicable to all. This problem tends to be rife within models of policy developed by American and British scholars but also appears for other nationalities as well. While the discussion of comparison above focused primarily on differences in political and policy cultures, institutional analysis also needs to be strengthened.

Some years ago Fritz Scharpf (1986) argued that policy design performed without references to the institutions within which that design is occurring is not likely to be successful. This argument and other institutionalist arguments are that design involves building institutional structures along with the policy (see House and Araral, 2013). That said, simple structural changes cannot be sufficient to guarantee policy successes, but rather these two aspects of policy need to be linked and constructed together.

The linkage between institutions and policy can be identified within a number of areas of the policy process. For example, the agenda-setting process is influenced by the number of available venues for getting issues in to the process. And implementation is shaped not only by the number of clearance points that may inhibit a policy being put into effect as planned but also the implementation structures that integrate public and private sector actors who affect the outcomes of the implementation process. We could extend the list of institutional linkages involved in making public policy function but the fundamental point is that policy cannot be considered in a structural or institutional vacuum.

Where do we go from here?

This book has provided a broad perspective on public policy. Although it has been written primarily from the perspective of political science and the political dimension of policy, I have attempted to include some perspectives from other disciplines. The book provides an overview of contemporary public policy analysis but there is still a great deal that needs to be done for policy analysis to fulfill the promise of improving the performance of governments and their allies in the private sector.

The design framework that I have been using for this volume is meant to provide a means of integrating a number of dimensions of policy analysis. The assumption is that by considering the cause of the perceived problem, the means of addressing that problem and the means of evaluating whether the interventions by the public sector have been successful it may be more possible to provide a clear understanding of how policies get made, and then remade. Further, by thinking of policymaking as a design process there is always a conception of what the final product should, or at least could, look like.

As committed as I may be to the general logic of policy design, this does not provide the detailed answers to many important questions. Those questions are in part academic but they are also practical. Scholars are interested in the theoretical and analytic questions associated with policy design, but a technology for effective policy design does not exist. Men and women involved in making policies for real governments with real people are less concerned with theory and more with whether a program will actually work. I have attempted to provide some insights for both of these communities, but the real answers for design come from blending the two stands of analysis and concern.

References

Alesina, A. and E.L. Glaser (2004) Fighting Poverty in the U.S. and Europe: A World of Difference (Oxford: Oxford University Press).

Alexander, E. (1984) "After rationality, what?: a review of responses to paradigm break-down", Journal of the American Planning Association 50, 62–9.

Alexander, E.R. (1989) "Improbable implementation: the Pressman-Wildavsky paradox revisited", Journal of Public Policy 9, 451–65.

Allison, G.T. and P. Zelikow (1999) The Essence of Decision, revised edn (New York: Longmans).

Alm, J. and B. Togler (2011) "Do ethics matter?: tax compliance and morality", Journal of Business Ethics 101, 635–61.

Alsott, A.L. (1995) "The earned income tax credit and the limitations of tax-based welfare policies", National Tax Journal 108, 533–92.

Army Corps of Engineers (1996) Risk-based Analysis for Corps Flood Project Studies (Davis, CA: Hydrological Engineering Center).

Arrow, K.J. (1996) Benefit-cost Analysis in Environmental Health and Safety Regulation (Washington, DC: Office of Management and Budget).

Auyero, J. (2012) Patients of the State: The Politics of Waiting in Argentina (Durham, NC: Duke University Press).

Axelrod, R. (2007) The Evolution of Cooperation, revised edn (New York: Basic Books).

Bache, I. (2013) "Measuring quality of life for public policy", European Journal of Public Policy 20, 21–38.

Bachrach, P. and M.S. Baratz (1962) "Two faces of power", American Political Science Review 56 (4), 947–52.

Bagenstos, S.R. (2000) "Subordination, stigma and 'disability'", Virginia Law Review 86, 398–486.

Baggott, R. (2012) "Policy success and public health: the case of public health in England", Journal of Social Policy 41, 391–408.

Baker, M. (2006) Restructuring Family Policy: Convergences and Divergences (Toronto: University of Toronto Press).

Bardach, E. (1977) The Implementation Game: What Happens After a Bill Becomes a Law (Cambridge, MA: MIT Press).

Bardach, E. (1998) Getting Agencies to Work Together: The Practice and Theory of Managerial Craftsmanship (Washington, DC: The Brookings Institution).

Bardach, E. and R. Kagan (1982) Going By the Book: The Problem of Regulatory Unreasonableness (Philadelphia, PA: Temple University Press).

Bardach, E. and R. Kagan (2009) Adversarial Legalism: The American Way of Law (Cambridge, MA: Harvard University Press).

Barrett, D. (2014) "Watchdog strips official status from police crime statistics", Telegraph, 15 January.

Bates, R.H., A. Greif, M. Levi, J.-L. Rosenthal and B.R. Weingast (1988) Analytic Narratives (Princeton, NJ: Princeton University Press).

Baumgartner, F.R. and B.D. Jones (2010) Agendas and Instability in American Politics, 2nd edn (Chicago, IL: University of Chicago Press).

Baumgartner, F.R., C. Breunig, C. Green-Pedersen et al. (2009) "Punctuated equilibrium in comparative perspective", American Journal of Political Science **53**, 603–20.

Beale, R. (1995) "Turf protection: conflict between authorities", Australian Journal of Public Administration **54**, 143–7.

Beland, D. (2010) "Reconsidering policy feedback: how policies affect politics", Administration and Society **42**, 568–90.

Bemelmans-Videc, M.-L., R.C. Rist and E. Vedung (1998) Carrots, Sticks and Sermons: Policy Instruments and their Evaluation (New Brunswick, NJ: Transaction Publishers).

Bennett, J.T. (2014) "Congressional conundrum: cut weapons programs now or later", Defense News, 11 May.

Benz, A. and J. Broschek (2012) Federal Dynamics: Continuity, Change and Varieties of Federalism (Oxford: Oxford University Press).

Bernstein, J. and S. Parrott (2014) Proposal to Strengthen Minimum Wage would Help Low-wage Workers, with Little Effect on Employment (Washington, DC: Center for Budget and Policy Priorities).

Best, R. (2010) "Situation or social problem: the influence of events on media coverage of the homeless", Social Problems **57**, 74–91.

Bingham, L.B., T. Nabatchi and R. O'Leary (2005) "The new governance: practices and processes for stakeholder and citizen participation in the work of government", Public Administration Review **65** (5), 547–58.

Birkland, T.A. (1998) "Focusing events, mobilization and agenda setting", Journal of Public Policy **18** (1), 53–74.

Birkland, T.A. (2006) Lessons from Disaster (Washington, DC: Georgetown University Press).

Birkland, T.A. and S.E. de Young (2013) "Focusing events and policy windows", in E. Araral, S. Fritzen, M. Howlett, M. Ramesh and X. Wu (eds), Routledge Handbook of Public Policy (London: Routledge).

Birkland, T.A. and S. Waterman (2008) "Is federalism the reason for policy failure in Hurricane Katrina", Publius **38**, 692–714.

Blatter, J. (2003) "Beyond hierarchies and networks: institutional logics and change in transboundary space", Governance **16**, 503–26.

Blaug, M. (2011) "Welfare economics", in R. Towse (ed.), Handbook of Cultural Economics (Cheltenham, UK and Northampton, MA, USA: Edward Elgar).

Blyth, M. (2007) "Puzzling, powering or persuading: the mechanisms for building institutional orders", International Studies Quarterly **51**, 761–77.

Bobrow, D. and J.S. Dryzek (1987) Policy Analysis by Design (Pittsburgh, PA: University of Pittsburgh Press).

Boin, A. (2004) "Lessons from crisis research", International Studies Quarterly **6**, 165–94.

Boin, A., P. 't Hart and B. Sundelius (2005) The Politics of Crisis Management: Public Leadership Under Pressure (Cambridge: Cambridge University Press).

Bok, S. (1978) Lying: Moral Choice in Public and Private Life (New York: Pantheon).

Boston, J., A. Braddock and D.L. Eng (2010) Public Policy: Why Ethics Matter (Canberra: ANU Press).

Botterill, L. (2013) "Turtles all the way down: bounded rationality in evidence-based policy analysis", Policy Sciences **33**, 367–79.

Bouckaert, G. and J.A. Halligan (2007) Managing Performance: International Comparisons (London: Routledge).

Bouckaert, G. and B.G. Peters (2002) "Performance measurement and management: the Achilles' heel of administrative modernization", Public Performance and Management Review **25**, 359–62.

Bovens, M.A.P. and P. 't Hart (1996) Understanding Policy Fiascoes (New Brunswick, NJ: Transaction Publishers).

Bovens, M.A.P., P. 't Hart and B.G. Peters (2000) Success and Failure in Public Governance (Cheltenham, UK and Northampton, MA, USA: Edward Elgar).

Bowen, E.B. (1982) "The Pressman-Wildavsky paradox: four addenda, or why models based on probability theory can predict implementation success and suggest useful tactical advice for implementers", Journal of Public Policy **2**, 1–21.

Braun, D. and F. Gilardi (2006) "Taking 'Galton's Problem' seriously: towards a theory of policy diffusion", Journal of Theoretical Politics **18**, 298–321.

Bressers, H. and P.J. Klok (1988) "Fundamentals for a theory of policy instruments", International Journal of Social Economics **15**, 22–41.

Brodkin, E.Z. (2011) "Policy work: street-level bureaucracy under the new managerialism", Journal of Public Administration Research and Theory **21**, 253–77.

Brook, Y. and D. Watkins (2010) Free Market Revolution (New York: Palgrave).

Brown, C. (2007) "Tragedy, tragic choices and contemporary international political theory", International Relations **21**, 5–13.

Browne, A. and A. Wildavsky (1984) "Implementation as adaptation", in J.L. Pressman and Wildavsky (eds), Implementation, 3rd edn (Berkeley, CA: University of California Press).

Calabrese, G. and P. Bobbitt (1978) Tragic Choices (New York: W.W. Norton).

Calista, D. (1994) "Policy implementation", in S. Nagel (ed.), Encyclopedia of Policy Studies, 2nd edn (New York: Marcel Dekker).

Capano, G. (2009) "Understanding policy change as an epistemological and theoretical challenge", Journal of Comparative Policy Analysis **11**, 7–31.

Carnes, N. (2013) White-collar Government: The Hidden Role of Class in Economic Policy-making (Chicago, IL: University of Chicago Press).

Carroll, A.E. (2014) "How Hobby Lobby rule could limit access to birth control", New York Times, 30 June.

Carter, P. (2012) "Policy as palimpsest", Policy and Politics **40**, 423–43.

Challis, L. (1988) Joint Approaches to Social Policy: Rationality and Practice (Cambridge: Cambridge University Press).

Chappell, L. (2002) "Federalism and social policy: the case of domestic violence", Australian Journal of Public Administration **60**, 59–69.

Chong, D. and J.N. Druckman (2007) "Framing theory", Annual Review of Political Science **10**, 103–26.

Christensen, T. and P. Laegreid (2007) Transcending New Public Management: The Transformation of Public Sector Reforms (Aldershot: Ashgate).

Clemmitt, M. (2014) "Can Obama's health insurance expansion recover from its shaky rollout?", CQ Researcher, 17 April.

Coady, C.A.J. (2010) "The problem of dirty hands", in Stanford Encyclopedia of Philosophy, http://stanford.library.usyd.edu.au/archives/win2010/entries/dirty-hands/ (accessed 20 December 2014).

Cobb, R.W. and C.D. Elder (1972) Participation in American Politics: The Dynamics of Agenda-building (Baltimore, MD: Johns Hopkins University Press).

Cohen, M.D., J.G. March and J.P. Olsen (1971) "A garbage can model of organizational choice", Administrative Science Quarterly **17**, 1–25.

Commonwealth Fund (2014) Mirror, Mirror on the Wall 2014 Update; How the US Health Care System Compares Internationally (New York: The Commonwealth Fund).

Considine, M. (2002) "The end of the line?: accountable governance in an age of networks, partnerships, and joined-up government", Governance **15** (1), 21–40.

Cook, B.J. (2010) "Arenas of power in climate change policy", Policy Studies Journal **39**, 465–86.

Culpepper, P.D. (2002) "Powering, puzzling and 'pacting': the informational logic of negotiated reforms", Journal of European Public Policy **9**, 774–90.

Dahl, P.S. and K.M. Hansen (2006) "Diffusion of standards: the importance of size, region and external pressures in diffusion processes", Public Administration **84**, 441–59.

Dahl, R.A. and C.E. Lindblom (1953) Politics, Economics and Welfare: Planning and Politico-economic Systems Resolved into Basic Processes (New York: Harper).

Dasgupta, P.S. and P.R. Ehrlich (2013) "Pervasive externalities at the population, consumption and environment nexus", Science **340**, 324–38.

Davis, O.A., M.A.H. Dempster and A. Wildavsky (1966) "A theory of the budgetary process", American Political Science Review **60** (3), 529–47.

Dempster, M.A.H. and A. Wildavsky (1979) "On change: or, there is no magic size for an increment", Political Studies **27**, 371–89.

Denhardt, R.B. and J.V. Denhardt (2007) The New Public Service: Serving Not Steering (Armonk, NY: M.E. Sharpe).

Dery, D. (2000) Agenda-Setting and Problem Definition, Policy Studies **21** (1), 27–47.

Doonan, M. (2013) American Federalism in Practice: The Formulation and Implementation of Contemporary Health Policy (Washington, DC: The Brookings Institution).

Downs, A. (1957) An Economic Theory of Democracy (New York: Harper).

Downs, A. (1972) "Up and down with ecology – the 'issue-attention cycle'", The Public Interest, 38–50.

Dror, Y. (1986) Policymaking Under Adversity (New Brunswick, NJ: Transaction Publishers).

Dubois, V. (2010) The Bureaucrat and the Poor: Encounters in a French Welfare Office (Aldershot: Ashgate).

Duit, A. and V. Galaz (2008) "Governance and complexity – new issues in governance theory", Governance 21, 311–35.

Dunlop. C. (2013) "Epistemic communities", in E. Araral, S. Fritzen, M. Howlett, M. Ramesh and X. Wu (eds), Routledge Handbook of Public Policy (London: Routledge).

Dunn, W.N. (2012) Public Policy Analysis: An Introduction (Boston, MA: Pearson).

Eckstein, H. (1980) The Natural History of Congruence Theory (Denver, CO: Graduate School of International Studies, University of Denver).

Elmore, R.F. (1985) "Forward and backward mapping: reversible logic in the analysis of public policy", in K. Hanf and T.A.J. Toonen (eds), Policy Implementation in Federal and Unitary States (Dordrecht: Martinus Nijhoff).

Elster, J. (1991) "The puzzling scope of rationality", European Journal of Sociology 32, 109–29.

Erler, H.A. (2013) "A new face of poverty: economic crises and poverty discourses", Poverty and Public Policy 4, 183–204.

Esping-Andersen, G. (1990) The Three Worlds of Welfare Capitalism (Princeton, NJ: Princeton University Press).

Eterno, J.A. and E.B. Silverman (2012) The Crime Numbers Game: Management by Manipulation (Boca Raton, FL: CRC Press).

Exworthy, M. and M. Powell (2004) "Big windows and little windows: implementation in the 'congested state'", Public Administration 82, 263–81.

Fancy, C. (2011) "The politics of social policy in America: the causes and effects of indirect versus direct social spending", Journal of Politics 73, 73–83.

Farrington, D.P. (2003) "British randomized experiments on crime and justice", Annals of the American Academy of Political and Social Sciences 589, 150–67.

Farrow, S. and R.O. Zerbe (2013) Principles and Standards for Cost-benefit Analysis (Cheltenham, UK and Northampton, MA, USA: Edward Elgar).

Feiock, R.C. (2013) "The institutional collective action framework", Policy Studies Journal 41, 397–425.

Fenna, A. and T.O. Hueglin (2006) Comparative Federalism: A Systematic Inquiry (Peterborough, Ontario: Broadview Press).

Fenner, F., D.A. Henderson, I. Arita, Z. Jezek and I.D. Ladnyi (1999) Smallpox and its Eradication (Geneva: World Health Organization).

Fernandez, S. and T. Moldogaziev (2011) "Empowering public sector employees: to improve performance; does it work?", American Review of Public Administration 4 (1), 23–47.

Ferrara, M. and M. Rhodes (2013) Recasting European Welfare States (London: Routledge).

Fischer, F. and H. Gottweiss (2012) The Argumentative Turn Revisited: Public Policy as Communicative Practice (Durham, NC: Duke University Press).

Forget, E.L. (2011) "The town with no poverty", Canadian Public Policy 37, 283–305.

Frederick, S., G. Loewenstein and T. O'Donoghue (2002) "Time discounting and time preference: a critical review", Journal of Economic Literature **40**, 351–401.

Freeman, G.P. (1985) "National styles and policy sectors: explaining structured variation", Journal of Public Policy **5** (4), 467–96.

Freeman, J.L. and J.P. Stevens (1987) "A theoretical and conceptual reexamination of subsystem politics", Public Policy and Administration **2**, 9–24.

Fugitt, D. and S.J. Wilcox (1999) Cost-benefit Analysis for Public Sector Decision Makers (Westport, CT: Quorum Books).

Fung, A., M. Graham and D. Weil (2007) Full Disclosure: The Perils and Promise of Transparency (Cambridge: Cambridge University Press).

Ganghof, S. (2003) "Promises and pitfalls of veto player analysis", Swiss Political Science Review **9**, 1–25.

Geva-May, I. (2004) "Riding the wave of opportunity: termination in public policy", Journal of Public Policy Research and Theory **14**, 309–33.

Gilley, B. (2009) The Right to Rule: How States Win and Lose Legitimacy (New York: Columbia University Press).

Gingrich, J.R. (2011) Making Markets in the Welfare State: The Politics of Varying Market Reforms (Cambridge: Cambridge University Press).

Glover, J. (1977) Causing Death and Saving Lives (London: Penguin).

Goodsell, C.T. (2011) Mission Mystique: Belief Systems in Public Agencies (Washington, DC: CQ Press).

Goodwin, P. and R.B. Noland (2003) "Building new roads really does create extra traffic", Applied Economics **35**, 1451–7.

Gormley, W.T. (1989) Taming the Bureaucracy: Muscles, Prayers and Other Strategies (Princeton, NJ: Princeton University Press).

Hadenius, A. and J. Toerell (2007) "Pathways from authoritarianism", Journal of Democracy **18**, 143–57.

Hahn, R.W. and C.R. Sunstein (2002) "A new executive order for improving federal regulation? Deeper and wider cost-benefit analysis", University of Pennsylvania Law Review **50**, 1489–552.

Hall, P.G. (1980) Great Planning Disasters (Berkeley, CA: University of California Press).

Halliburton, R. (2014) Autonomy and the Situated Self: A Challenge to Bioethics (Lanham, MD: Lexington Books).

Hammerschmid, G. and R. Meyer (2004) "Public management dynamics in a federal legalistic Rechtstaat: results from an executive survey in Austria", International Journal of Public Sector Management **18**, 629–40.

Hammersley, M. (2013) The Myth of Research-based Policy and Practice (London: Sage).

Handler, J.F. and Y. Hasenfeld (2006) Blame Welfare: Ignore Poverty and Inequality (New York: Cambridge University Press).

Hanf, K. and T.A.J. Toonen (1985) Policy Implementation in Federal and Unitary States (Dordrecht: Martinus Nijhoff).

Hausman, D.M. and B. Welch (2010) "Debate; to nudge or not to nudge", Journal of Political Philosophy **18**, 123–36.

Hayes, M.T. (2006) Incrementalism and Public Policy (Lanham, MD: University Press of America).

Heclo, H. (1974) Modern Social Politics in Britain and Sweden (New Haven, CT: Yale University Press).

Helms, L. (2012) Poor Leadership and Bad Governance (Cheltenham, UK and Northampton, MA, USA: Edward Elgar).

Hemerijck, A. (2012) Changing Welfare States (Oxford: Oxford University Press).

Henry, A.D. (2011a) "Information, networks and complexity of trust in commons governance", International Journal of the Commons 5, 188–212.

Henry, A.D. (2011b) "Ideology, power and the structure of policy networks", Policy Studies Journal 39, 361–83.

Hepburn, C. (2007) "Valuing the far-off future: discounting and its alternatives", in G. Atkinson, S. Dietz and E. Neumayer (eds), Handbook of Sustainable Development (Cheltenham, UK and Northampton, MA, USA: Edward Elgar).

Héritier, A. and M. Rhodes (eds) (2012) New Modes of Governance in Europe: Governing in the Shadow of Hierarchy (Basingstoke: Palgrave).

Hill, M. and P. Hupe (2014) Implementing Public Policy, 3rd edn (London: Sage).

Hisschemöller, M. and R. Hoppe (1995) "Coping with intractable controversies: the case of problem structuring in policy design and analysis", Knowledge and Policy 8, 40–60.

Hjern, B. and D.O. Porter (1981) "Implementation structures: a new unit of administrative analysis", Organization Studies, 2 (3), 211–27.

Ho, L.-S. (2011) Public Policy and the Public Interest (London: Routledge).

Hogwood, B.W. and B.G. Peters (1983) Policy Dynamics (Brighton: Wheatsheaf).

Hood, C. (1976) The Tools of Government (Chatham, NJ: Chatham House).

Hood, C. (2011) The Blame Game: Spin, Bureaucracy and Self-preservation in Government (Princeton, NJ: Princeton University Press).

Hood, C. and H. Margetts (2007) Tools of Government in a Digital Age (Basingstoke: Macmillan).

Hooghe, L. and G. Marks (2003) "Unraveling the central state, but how? Types of multi-level governance", American Political Science Review 103, 233–43.

Hoppe, R. (2010) The Governance of Problems: Puzzling, Powering and Participation (Bristol: Policy Press).

Houghton, D.P. (1998) "Analogical reasoning and policymaking: where and when is it used?", Policy Sciences 31, 151–76.

House, R.S and E. Araral (2013) "The institutional analysis and development framework", in E. Araral, S. Fritzen, M. Howlett, M. Ramesh and X. Wu (eds), Routledge Handbook of Public Policy (London: Routledge).

Howlett, M. (2001) Designing Public Policy: Principles and Instruments (London: Routledge).

Howlett, M. and R.P. Lejano (2013) "Tales from the crypt: the rise and fall (and rebirth?) of policy design", Administration and Society 45, 357–81.

Howlett, M. and J. Rayner (2007) "Design principles for policy mixes: cohesion and coherence in 'new governance arrangements'", Policy and Society 26, 1–18.

Hupe, P. (2007) "The policy cycle", in B.G. Peters and J. Pierre (eds), Handbook of Public Policy (London: Sage).

Hupe, P. and A. Buffat (2014) "A public service gap: capturing contexts in a comparative approach to street level bureaucracy", Public Management Review **16** (4), 548–69.

Ingram, H.B and A.L. Schneider (1990) "Improving implementation through framing smarter statutes", Journal of Public Policy **10**, 61–87.

Interorganizational Committee (2003) "Principles and guidelines for social impact assessment in the USA", Impact Assessment and Project Appraisal **21**, 231–50.

Isaacs, D., H. Kilham, J. Leask and B. Tobin (2009) "Ethical issues in vaccination", Vaccine **27**, 615–18.

Jacobs, A.M. (2011) Governing in the Long Term: Democracy and the Politics of Investment (Cambridge: Cambridge University Press).

Jacobs, L.R. and T. Skocpol (2005) Inequality and American Democracy: What We Know and What We Need to Learn (New York: Russell Sage Foundation).

James, T.E. and P.D. Jorgensen (2009) "Policy knowledge, policy formulation, and change: revisiting a foundational question", Policy Studies Journal **37**, 141–62.

Jann, W. and K. Weigrich (2007) "Theories of the policy process", in F. Fischer, G.J. Miller and M.S. Sidney (eds), Handbook of Public Policy Analysis (Boca Raton, FL: CRC Press).

Jay, S., C. Jones, P. Slinn and C. Wood (2007) "Environmental impact assessment: retrospect and prospect", Environmental Impact Assessment Review **27**, 287–300.

Jenkins-Smith, H.C. and P.A. Sabatier (1999) "The advocacy coalition framework: an assessment", in P.A. Sabatier (ed.), Theories of the Policy Process (Boulder, CO: Westview Press).

John, P. (2013) "All tools are informational: how information and persuasion define the tools of government", Policy and Politics **41**, 605–20.

Jones, B.D. (2001) Politics and the Architecture of Choice: Bounded Rationality and Governance (Chicago, IL: University of Chicago Press).

Jones, B.D and F.R. Baumgartner (2012) "From there to here: punctuated equilibrium to the general punctuation thesis to a theory of government information processing", Policy Studies Journal **40**, 1–20.

Jones, C.O. (1984) An Introduction to the Study of Public Policy, 2nd edn (Monterey, CA: Brooks-Cole).

Kerwin, C.M. (2011) Rule-making: How Government Agencies Write Law and Make Policy, 4th edn (Washington, DC: CQ Press).

Kingdon, J.W. (1985) Agendas, Alternatives and Public Policies (New York: Longman), reprinted in 2003.

Kirschen, E.S. (1964) Economic Policy in Our Time (Amsterdam: North-Holland).

Kiser, L.L. and E. Ostrom (2000) "The three worlds of action: a metatheoretical synthesis of institutional approaches", in M.D. McGinnis (ed.), Polycentric Games and Institutions: Readings from the Workshop in Political Theory (Ann Arbor, MI: University of Michigan Press).

Krugman, P. (2014) "The myth of German austerity", New York Times, February 23.

Laegreid, P. and K. Verhoest (2010) Governance of Public Sector Organizations: Proliferation, Autonomy, and Performance (Basingstoke: Macmillan).

Landry, R., M. Lamari and N. Amara (2003) "The extent and determinants of the utilization of university research in government agencies", Public Administration Review **63**, 192–205.

Lane, J.-E. (1983) "The concept of implementation", Statsvetenskapliga Tidskrift 17–40.

Lascoumbes, P. (2011) "L'action publique au prisme de ses instruments", Revue française de science politique **61**, 5–22.

Lascoumbes, P. and P. Le Gales (2007) "Understanding public policy through its instruments – from the nature of instruments to the sociology of public policy instrumentation", Governance **20**, 1–21.

Lasswell, H.D. (1936) Politics: Who Gets What When, How (New York: McGraw-Hill).

Lasswell, H.D. (1956) The Decision Process; Seven Categories of Functional Analysis (College Park, MD: College of Business and Public Administration, University of Maryland).

Lerner, D. and H.D. Lasswell (1951) The Policy Sciences (Palo Alto, CA: Stanford University Press).

Levi, M. (1997) Consent, Dissent and Patriotism (Cambridge: Cambridge University Press).

Levin, K., B. Cashore, S. Bernstein and G. Auld (2010) "Playing it forward: path dependency, progressive incrementalism and the 'super wicked' problem of climate change", Unpublished paper.

Levin, K., B. Cashore, S. Bernstein and G. Auld (2012) "Overcoming the tragedy of super wicked problems: constraining our future selves to ameliorate global climate change", Policy Sciences **45**, 121–52.

Lijphart, A. (1984) Democracies: Patterns of Majoritarian and Consensus Government in Twenty-one Countries (New Haven, CT: Yale University Press).

Lindblom, C.E. (1965) The Intelligence of Democracy: Decision Making Through Mutual Adjustment (New York: Free Press).

Linder, S.H. and B.G. Peters (1984) "From social theory to policy design", Journal of Public Policy **4**, 237–59.

Linder, S.H. and B.G. Peters (1987) "A design perspective on policy implementation: the fallacy of misplaced precision", Review of Policy Research **6**, 459–75.

Linder, S.H. and B.G. Peters (1989) "Instruments of government: perceptions and contexts", Journal of Public Policy **9**, 35–58.

Lipsky, M. (1980) Street-level Bureaucracy: Dilemmas of the Individual in Public Services (New York: Russell Sage).

Lowi, T.J. (1964) "American business, public policy, case studies and political theory", World Politics **16**, 677–715.

Lowi, T.J. (1972) "Four systems of politics, policy and choice", Public Administration Review **32**, 298–310.

Lukes, S. (2004) Power: A Radical View, 2nd edn (Basingstoke: Palgrave Macmillan).

Lundqvist, L. (1980) The Hare and the Tortoise: Clean Air Policies in the United States and Sweden (Ann Arbor, MI: University of Michigan Press).

Macdonald, D. (2001) "Coerciveness and the selection of environmental policy instruments", Canadian Public Administration **44**, 161–87.

Macdonald, R. (2005) "The Swiss army knife of government", in P. Eliadis, M. Hill and M. Howlett (eds), Designing Government (Montreal: McGill/Queens University Press).

MacMahan, J. (2006) The Ethics of Killing: Problems at the Margin of Life (Oxford: Oxford University Press).

Madrick, J. (2009) The Case for Big Government (Princeton, NJ: Princeton University Press).

Mahoney, J. and K. Thelen (2010) Explaining Institutional Change: Ambiguity, Agency and Power (Cambridge: Cambridge University Press).

Majone, G. (2001) "Nonmajoritarian institutions and the limits of democratic governance: a political transaction-cost approach", Journal of Institutional and Theoretical Economics 157, 57–78.

Majone, G. (2002a) "The precautionary principle and its policy implications", Journal of Common Market Studies 40, 89–109.

Majone, G. (2002b) Regulating Europe (London: Routledge).

Maor, M. (2013) "Policy bubbles: policy overreaction and positive feedback", Governance 27, 469–87.

March, J.G. and J.P. Olsen (1989) Rediscovering Institutions: The Organizational Basis of Politics (New York: Free Press).

Marier, P. (2013) "Policy learning", in E. Araral, S. Fritzen, M. Howlett. M. Ramesh and X. Wu (eds), Routledge Handbook of Public Policy (London: Routledge).

Marshall, T.H. (1964) Class, Citizenship and Social Development (Garden City, NY: Doubleday).

May, P.J. (1992) "Policy failure and learning", Journal of Public Policy 12, 187–206.

May, P.J. and A.E. Jochim (2013) "Policy regime perspective: policies, politics and governing", Policy Studies Journal 39, 285–305.

May, P.J., A.E. Jochim and B. Pump (2010) "Boundary-spanning policy problems: politics and policymaking", Paper presented at the Annual Meeting of the American Political Science Association, Washington, DC.

Maynard-Mooney, S. and M. Musheno (2003) Cops, Teachers, Counselors: Narratives on Street-level Judgment (Ann Arbor, MI: University of Michigan Press).

McConnell, A. (2010) Understanding Policy Success: Rethinking Public Policy (Basingstoke: Macmillan).

McCool, D. (1998) "The subsytem family of concepts: a critique and a proposal", Political Research Quarterly 51, 551–70.

McCubbins, M.D., R. Noll and B. Weingast (1989) "Structure and process, politics and policy: administrative arrangements and the political control of agencies", Virginia Law Review 75, 431–82.

McDonnell, L.M and R.F. Elmore (1987) "Getting the job done: alternative policy instruments", Educational Evaluation and Policy Analysis 9, 133–52.

McElroy, D. (2013) "UN warning over legal 'designer drugs'", Telegraph, 16 December.

McFarland, A.S. (2004) Neopluralism: The Evolution of Political Process Theory (Lawrence, KS: University Press of Kansas).

McKibbin, W.J. (2007) "The economics of international policy coordination", Economic Record 64, 241–53.

Meltsner, A.J. (1972) "Political feasibility and policy analysis", Public Administration Review **32**, 859–67.

Merton, R.K. (1936) "The unanticipated consequences of purposive social action", American Sociological Review **1**, 894–904.

Mishan, E.J. and E. Quah (2007) Cost-benefit Analysis, 5th edn (London: Routledge).

Mitchell, R.C. and R.T. Carson (2013) Using Surveys to Value Public Goods (London: Routledge).

Molina, O. and M. Rhodes (2002) "Corporatism: the past, present and future of a concept", Annual Review of Political Science **5**, 305–31.

Moore, M.A., A.E. Boardman, A.R. Vining, D.L. Weimer and D.H. Greenberg (2004) "'Just give me the number!': practical values for the social discount rate", Journal of Public Policy Analysis and Management **23**, 789–812.

Morag-Levine, N. (2009) Chasing the Wind: Regulating Air Pollution in the Common Law State (Princeton, NJ: Princeton University Press).

Mörth, U. (2004) Soft Law in Governance and Regulation: An Interdisciplinary Analysis (Cheltenham, UK and Northampton, MA, USA: Edward Elgar).

Mucciaroni, G. (2013) "The garbage can model and the politics of policymaking", in E. Araral, S. Fritzen, M. Howlett. M. Ramesh and X. Wu (eds), Routledge Handbook of Public Policy (London: Routledge).

Mulley, A., J. Wennberg, J. Weinstein, E. Fisher and A. Binagawho (2013) "Embracing delivery science for universal health care", The Lancet **382**, 25–6.

Musgrave, R.A. (1957) "A multiple theory of budget determination", FinanzArchiv **25**, 33–43.

Nelson, B.J. (1984) Making an Issue of Child Abuse: Political Agenda-setting for Social Problems (Chicago, IL: University of Chicago Press).

Nelson, R.R. (1977) The Moon and the Ghetto (New York: W.W. Norton).

North, D.C. (1993) "Institutions and credible commitment", Journal of Institutional and Theoretical Economics **149**, 11–23.

Nowrasteh, A. and S. Cole (2014) Building a Wall Around the Welfare State, Not the Country (Washington, DC: Cato Institute).

O'Riordan, T. and J. Cameron (2013) Interpreting the Precautionary Principle (London: Routledge).

O'Sullivan, A. and K. Gibb (2003) Housing Economics and Public Policy (Oxford: Blackwell Scientific).

O'Toole, L.J. (2000) "Research on policy implementation: assessments and prospects", Journal of Public Administration Research and Theory **10**, 263–88.

O'Toole, L.J. (2011) "Interorganization relations in implementation", in B.G. Peters and J. Pierre (eds), Handbook of Public Administration, 2nd edn (London: Sage).

OECD (Organisation for Economic Co-operation and Development) (2010) Regulatory Policy and Sustainable Growth (Paris: OECD).

Ostrom, E. (1990) Governing the Commons: The Evolution of Institutions of Collective Action (Cambridge: Cambridge University Press).

Ostrom, E. and X. Basurto (2011) "Crafting analytical tools to study institutional change", Journal of Institutional Economics **7**, 317–43.

Otsuki, T., J.S. Wilson and M. Sawedeh (2001) "Saving two in a billion: quantifying the trade effects of European food safety standards on African exports", Food Policy **26**, 496–514.

Pawson, R. (2006) Evidence-based Policy: A Realist Perspective (London: Sage).

Payan, T. (2006) Cops, Soldiers and Diplomats: Explaining Agency Behavior in the War on Drugs (Lanham, MD: Lexington Books).

Perrow, C. (1984) Normal Accidents: Living with High Risk Technologies (New York: Basic Books).

Peters, B.G. (2001a) The Future of Governing: Four Emerging Models, revised edn (Lawrence, KS: University Press of Kansas).

Peters, B.G. (2001b) "The politics of policy instruments", in L.M. Salamon (ed.), Handbook of Policy Instruments (New York: Oxford University Press).

Peters, B.G. (2007) "Performance-based accountability", in A. Shah (ed.), Performance Accountability and Combating Corruption (Washington, DC: World Bank).

Peters, B.G. (2014a) Pursuing Horizontal Management: The Politics of Public Sector Coordination (Lawrence, KS: University Press of Kansas).

Peters, B.G. (2014b) "Implementation structures as institutions", Public Policy and Administration **29**, 84–105.

Peters, B.G. (2015, forthcoming) American Public Policy: Promise and Performance, 10th edn (Washington, DC: CQ Press).

Peters, B.G. and J. Hoornbeek (2005) "The problem of policy problems", in P. Eliadis, M. Hill and M. Howlett (eds), Designing Government (Montreal: McGill/Queens University Press).

Peters, B.G. and J. Pierre (2013) "Food policy as a wicked problem", World Food Policy Journal (Bangkok) **1**.

Peters, B.G., E. Schröter and P. von Maravić (2013) The Politics of Representative Bureaucracy (Cheltenham, UK and Northampton, MA, USA: Edward Elgar).

Petridou, E. (2014) "Theories of the policy process: contemporary scholarship and future directions", Policy Studies Journal **42** (S1), S12–S32.

Pierre, J. (2011) The Politics of Urban Governance (Basingstoke: Macmillan).

Pierre, J. (2014) "Can urban regimes travel in time and space?", Urban Affairs Review **10**, 85–102.

Piven, F.F. and R.A. Cloward (1993) Regulating the Poor, 2nd edn (New York: Vintage).

Pollitt, C. (2013) "The logics of performance management", Evaluation **19**, 346–63.

Pollitt, C. and C. Talbot (2004) Unbundled Government: A Critical Analysis of Global Trend to Agencies, Quangos and Contractualization (London: Routledge).

Posner, E.A. and A. Vermeule (2003) "Reparations for slavery and other historical injustices", Columbia Law Review **103**, 689–748.

Pralle, S.B. (2003) "Venue shopping, political strategy and policy change: the internationalization of Canadian forest advocacy", Journal of Public Policy **23**, 233–60.

Pressman, J.L. and A. Wildavsky (1974) Implementation (Berkeley, CA: University of California Press).

Quill, T.E. (2005) "Terri Schiavo – a tragedy compounded", New England Journal of Medicine, **352**, 1630–33.

Rachels, J. (1986) The End of Life: Euthanasia and Mortality (Oxford: Oxford University Press).

Radaelli, C. (2009) "Measuring policy learning: regulatory impact assessment in Europe", Journal of European Public Policy **16**, 1145–64.

Radin, B. (2006) Challenging the Performance Movement: Accountability, Complexity and Democratic Values (Washington, DC: Georgetown University Press).

Rawlinson, K. (2013) "Police crime figures being manipulated, admits Chief Inspector", Guardian, 18 December.

Rawls, J. (1971) A Theory of Justice (Cambridge, MA: Harvard University Press).

Rawls, J. (2001) Justice as Fairness: A Restatement (Cambridge, MA: Harvard University Press).

Rhodes, M. (2001) "The political economy of social pacts: 'competitive corporatism' and European welfare reform", in P. Pierson (ed.), The New Politics of the Welfare State (Oxford: Oxford University Press).

Richardson, J.J. (1982) Policy Styles in Western Europe (London: Allen and Unwin).

Rittel, H.W.J. and M.M. Webber (1973) "Dilemmas in the general theory of planning", Policy Sciences **4**, 155–69.

Robinson, S.E. and K.J. Meier (2006) "Path dependence and organizational behavior – bureaucracy and social promotion", American Review of Public Administration **36** (3), 241–60.

Rose, R. (1993) Lesson-drawing in Public Policy: A Guide to Learning Across Time and Space (Chatham, NJ: Chatham House).

Rose-Ackerman, S. (1996) Controlling Environmental Policy: The Limits of Public Law in Germany and the United States (New Haven, CT: Yale University Press).

Rossi, P.H., M.W. Lipsey and H.E. Freeman (2004) Evaluation: A Systematic Approach, 7th edn (Thousand Oaks, CA: Sage).

Sabatier, P.A. and H. Jenkins-Smith (1999) "The advocacy-coalition framework: an assessment", in P.A. Sabatier (ed.), Theories of the Policy Process (Boulder, CO; Westview Press).

Saetren, H. (2014) "Implementing the third generation research in policy implementation research: an empirical assessment", Public Policy and Administration **29**, 84–105.

Salamon, L.M. (1979) "The time dimension in policy evaluation: the case of New Deal land reform", Public Policy **27**, 129–83.

Salamon, L.M. (2001a) Handbook of Policy Instruments (New York: Oxford University Press).

Salamon, L.M. (2001b) "Introduction", in L.M. Salamon (ed.), Handbook of Policy Instruments (New York: Oxford University Press).

Sandmo, A. (2000) The Public Economics of the Environment (Oxford: Oxford University Press).

Scharpf, F.W. (1986) "Policy failure and institutional reform: why should form follow function", International Social Science Journal **38**, 179–89.

Scharpf, F.W. (1988) "The joint decision trap: lessons from German federalism and European integration", Public Administration **66**, 239–78.

Scharpf, F.W. (1997) Games Real Actors Play: Actor-centered Institutionalism in Policy Research (Boulder, CO: Westview Press).

Scharpf. F.W. (2009) "Legitimacy in the multilevel European polity", European Political Science Review **1**, 173–94.

Schattschneider, E.E. (1962) The Semi-sovereign People (New York: Holt, Rinehart and Winston).

Schneider, A.L. (2013) "Policy design and transfer", in E. Araral, S. Fritzen, M. Howlett, M. Ramesh and X. Wu (eds), Routledge Handbook of Public Policy (London: Routledge).

Schneider, A. and H. Ingram (1988) "Systematically pinching ideas: a comparative approach to policy design", Journal of Public Policy **8**, 61–80.

Schneider, A. and H. Ingram (1993) "Social construction of target populations: implications for politics and policy", American Political Science Review **87**, 334–47.

Schön, D.A. and M. Rein (1994) Frame Reflection: Solving Intractable Policy Disputes (New York: Basic Books).

Schulman, P.R. (1980) Large-scale Policymaking (New York: Elsevier-North Holland).

Schwartz, J.E. (1987) America's Hidden Success: A Reassessment of Twenty Years of Public Policy (New York: W.W. Norton).

Scriven, M. (1991) "Prose and cons about goal free evaluation", American Journal of Evaluation **12**, 55–62.

Self, P. (1975) Econocrats and the Policy Process: Nonsense on Stilts (London: Macmillan).

Sen, A. (2009) The Idea of Justice (Cambridge, MA: Harvard University Press).

Shirley, M. (2008) Institutions and Development (Cheltenham, UK and Northampton, MA, USA: Edward Elgar).

Sieber, S. (1980) Fatal Remedies: Dilemmas of Social Intervention (New York: Plenum).

Simon, H.A. (1947) Administrative Behavior (New York: Free Press).

Simpson, D. and J. Walker (1987) "Extending cost-benefit analysis for energy investment choices", Energy Policy **15**, 217–27.

Skocpol, T. (1992) Protecting Soldiers and Mothers: The Political Origins of Social Policy in the United States (Cambridge, MA: Belknap Press).

Slemrod, J. (2007) "Cheating ourselves: the economics of tax evasion", Journal of Economic Perspectives **21**, 25–48.

Slovic, P. (2000) The Perception of Risk (London: Earthscan).

Somashekar, S. and J. Millman (2014) "Obamacare enrollment reaches 7.5 million", Washington Post, 10 April.

Sørenson, E. and J. Torfing (2007) Theories of Democratic Network Governance (Basingstoke: Macmillan).

Stigler, G.J. (1972) "The law and economics of public policy: a plea to the scholars", Journal of Legal Studies **1**, 1–18.

Stoker, R.P. (1991) Reluctant Partners: Implementing Federal Policy (Pittsburgh, PA: University of Pittsburgh Press).

Stone, D.A. (1997) Policy Paradox: The Art of Political Decision-making (New York: W.W. Norton).

Stone, D.A. (2002) Policy Paradox: The Art of Political Decision-making, revised edn (New York: W.W. Norton).

Sum, N.-L. and B. Jessop (2013) "Competitiveness, the knowledge-based economy, and higher education", Journal of the Knowledge Economy **4**, 24–44.

Sumalia, U.R. and C. Walters (2005) "Intergenerational discounting: an intuitive approach", Ecological Economics **52**, 135–42.

Sunstein, C.R. (2013) "The value of statistical life: some clarifications and puzzles", Journal of Benefit-Cost Analysis **4**, 247–61.

Sunstein, C.R. (2014) Valuing Life: Humanizing the Regulatory State (Chicago, IL: University of Chicago Press).

Taylor, S. (1984) Making Bureaucracies Think: The Environmental Impact Statement Strategy of Administrative Reform (Palo Alto, CA: Stanford University Press).

Termeer, C., A. Dewulf and M. Van Lieshout (2010) "Disentangling scale approaches in governance research: comparing monocentric, multilevel and adaptive governance", Ecology and Society **15**, 29–46.

Thalen, R.W. and C.R. Sunstein (2008) Nudge: Improving Decisions About Health, Wealth and Happiness (New Haven, CT: Yale University Press).

The Economist (2013) "Slavery reparations: blood money", 5 October.

Thompson, D.F. (1999) "Democratic secrecy", Political Science Quarterly **114**, 181–93.

Torfing, J., B.G. Peters, J. Pierre and E. Sørensen (2012) Interactive Governance: Advancing the Paradigm (Oxford: Oxford University Press).

Truog, R.D. (2008) "Consent for organ donations – balancing conflicting ethical obligations", New England Journal of Medicine **358**, 1209–11.

Tsebelis, G. (2000) Veto Players: How Political Institutions Work (Princeton, NJ: Princeton University Press).

UNICEF (2005) The "Rights" Start to Life: A Statistical Analysis of Birth Registration (New York: UNICEF).

Van Dooren, W., G. Bouckaert and J.A. Halligan (2010) Performance Management in the Public Sector (London: Routledge).

Van Hulst, M. and D. Yanow (2014) "From policy 'frames' to 'framing': theorizing a more dynamic, political approach", American Review of Public Administration, 30 May, http://arp.sagepub.com/content/early/2014/05/28/0275074014533142.

Vanderbroght, Y. and S. Yamasaki (2004) "Des cas logiques ... contradictoires", Revue internationale de politique compareé **11**, 51–66.

Vedung, E. (2007) "Policy evaluation", in B.G. Peters and J. Pierre (eds), Handbook of Public Policy (London: Sage).

Vedung, E. (2010) "Four waves of evaluation diffusion", Evaluation **16**, 263–77.

Vedung, E. (2013) "Six models of evaluation", in E. Araral, S. Fritzen, M. Howlett, M. Ramesh and X. Wu (eds), Routledge Handbook of Public Policy (London: Routledge).

Visser. J. (2007) "Deutero-learning in organizations: a review and a reformulation", Academy of Management Review **32**, 659–67.

Wald, M.L. (2012) "Court backs E.P.A. over emissions limits intended to reduce global warming", New York Times, 26 June.

Walker, J. (1977) "Setting the agenda in the US Senate: a theory of problem selection", British Journal of Political Science **7**, 423–56.

Wallis, J. and B. Dollery (1999) Market Failure, Government Failure, Leadership and Public Policy (New York: St Martin's Press).

Walzer, M. (1973) "Political action: the problem of dirty hands", Philosophy and Public Affairs 2, 160–80.

Weaver, R.K. and B.A. Rockman (1993) Do Institutions Matter? Government Capabilities in the United States and Abroad (Washington, DC: The Brookings Institution).

Weber, E.U. and P.C. Stern (2011) "Public understanding of climate change in the United States", American Psychologist 66, 315–28.

Weimer, D.L. (1993) "The current state of design craft: borrowing, tinkering and problem solving", Public Administration Review 53, 110–20.

Whittington, D. and D. MacRae Jr (1996) "The issue of standing in cost-benefit analysis", Journal of Policy Analysis and Management 5, 665–82.

Wilson, J.Q. (1980) The Politics of Regulation (New York: Basic Books).

Wilson, R. and E.A.C. Crouch (2001) Risk-benefit Analysis (Cambridge, MA: Center for Risk Analysis, Harvard University).

Winter, S. (2011) "The implementation perspective", in B.G. Peters and J. Pierre (eds), Handbook of Public Administration, 2nd edn (London: Sage).

Wolf, C. (1987) "Market and non-market failures: comparison and assessment", Journal of Public Policy 7, 43–70.

Workman, S., B.D. Jones and A.E. Jochim (2009) "Information processing and policy dynamics", Policy Studies Journal 37, 75–92.

Xue, J. (2012) Growth With Inequality: An International Comparison on Income Inequality (Singapore: World Scientific Publishers).

Zaharadias, N. (2014) "Bounded rationality and garbage-can models of policymaking", in P. Zittoun and B.G. Peters (eds), Contemporary Approaches to Policymaking (London and New York: Palgrave Macmillan).

Zito, A. (2001) "Epistemic communities, collective entrepreneurship and European integration", Journal of European Public Policy 8, 585–603.

Zito, A.R. and A. Schout (2009) "Learning theory reconsidered: EU integration theories and learning", European Journal of Public Policy 16, 1103–23.

Zubriggen, C. (forthcoming) "Governance in Latin America", Policy and Society.

Index